MINUTES OF THE LAST MEETING

Above: John Decker and his wife, Phyllis, in the Bundy Drive studio *(photo by Jack Wilkes)*

Below: John Decker, Gene Fowler, and John Barrymore, with the dachshund Gus, looking on at a chess game in the Decker studio *(photo by Charles Rhodes, copyright, Fawcett Publications, Inc.)*

GENE FOWLER

———

Minutes

of the

Last

Meeting

———

THE VIKING PRESS, NEW YORK

1954

LIBRARY OF CONGRESS CATALOG CARD NUMBER: 54-6425

PRINTED IN THE UNITED STATES OF AMERICA
AMERICAN BOOK—STRATFORD PRESS, INC., NEW YORK

To PASCAL COVICI
Veteran friend and incurable confidant

For no one, in our long decline,
So dusty, spiteful and divided,
Had quite such pleasant friends as mine,
Or loved them half as much as I did.

—Hilaire Belloc

MINUTES OF THE LAST MEETING

---

*The only imperfect thing in nature
is the human race.*
                              —Sadakichi

From a window of the hillside shed in which I work I
see a California blue jay. The bird thrusts at a peach with
the precision of a fencing master. The last peach of mid-
August ripens upon a tree almost lost among its random
neighbors—the alien eucalyptus and a miscellany of native
evergreens—on the floor of the glen below me.

It is a chance marriage of strong colors: the electric blue
of the bird's wings, its slate-blue breast, and the rose-yellow
blaze of the peach against forest green. To recollect in art
anything comparable to this exuberance of nature one thinks
back to the Indians of mountain and plain, the Utes, the
Sioux, or the mesa folk, who improvised upon their buck-
skins and their gourds, or in textiles and clays, and antici-
pated Picasso and Modigliani with ceremonial abstractions
upon their faces and bodies. Echoes of the rainbow are best

[3]

observed by primitive man, by a genius, or by some lovely child.

Daily from my gallery I watch the cloak-and-dagger play of nature's smaller actors against a proscenium of trees. When a military airplane flies low overhead, the birds flee off-stage, as though quite aware of that modern violence which is charged and triggered against peaceful creatures.

Notwithstanding the powder burns of older wars, there was a time when dread did not monopolize our waking hours, nor terror cancel out our sleep. The days come up as though on a great conveyor belt, and drop round and under and into the past. A mysterious gentleman in red boots (I believe he is a master barber by profession) stands nearby to call out "Next!" And I see my good companions go one by one beyond the narrow door.

I do not yield to loneliness; instead I brighten as I recall the yesterdays at the studio of the artist John Decker on Bundy Drive. That brown-beamed studio was a place of meeting for still-lively survivors of bohemian times, an artists' Alamo, where political bores never intruded and where breast-beating hypocrites could find no listeners. The men seen most often at the Bundy Drive studio had been, or now were, persons of mark; yet never long-haired nor precious nor hoodwinked by false prophets who fed upon weeds of the sea. These men lived intensely, as do children and poets and jaguars.

John Decker was, in a roguish fashion, childlike; he was talented at the easel and a superb cook. This unpredictable fellow disliked sunsets and his dead mother. There was much mischief in him but no malice. A creature of caprice, he had a most generous heart. He was overfond of gold trinkets, unsalted butter, brass artifacts; of Van Gogh's canvases, maroon dinner jackets, and spirited comrades. John Decker was no saint, nor were his cronies.

Our friend had turns of exaggerated self-interest—the occupational disease of many artists. At other times it seemed as though his insides were exposed and spilled across the plywood boards upon which he mostly painted in preference to the stretched canvas. When in this mood Decker would show compassion for the unwanted ones who hunger for affection as well as for bread. If ill or penniless (the two misfortunes he most frequently endured), or cast down with recollections, Decker seldom groaned, but swore instead; an indication of defiance, and, to my way of thinking, the proper mark of an artist, who never should be a good loser.

The consecrated workers in pigment or stone dare not smile upon their adversaries or make over-modest appraisals of their own powers. The artistic woods are full of censors eager to accept and magnify a derogatory word. Failure of the old sweet-singing bards to profess their own virtues hastened their downfall; and now we have small poetry, and have grown tone-deaf, and demented by propaganda; and hatred has become a science; envy, a religion.

There at the Bundy Drive studio John Barrymore used to sit in an antique chair upholstered in frayed red velour, a chair that long ago had belonged to Rudolph Valentino at Falcon's Lair. To that room came actor Thomas Mitchell, a collector of good paintings and of good friends; actors Norman Kerry, Roland Young, Vincent Price, Anthony Quinn, Alan Mowbray; John Carradine, his long thin jaw

wagging in iambic pentameter; Philip Paval, a clever worker
in silver and gold; the mercurial Errol Flynn; author Ben
Hecht; and occasionally an introspective sculptor whose
name I forget, but who, according to his legend, had fur-
thered his knowledge of anatomy by dissecting his dead
father. He presently was having recourse to psychoanalysis
to rid him of the desire to punch his wife's nose. All these
hearties, as well as several older persons of lapsed fame, met
at John Decker's studio from time to time, quite informally
indeed, to eat, drink, and pursue a glad continuance of life
left over from their summer years.

Here also the squirelike face and red-veined nose of comedian W. C. Fields shone in the light of studio lamps. He
would grow louder and ruddier at some real or fancied
affront, as on the day when an insurance company declined
to renew his accident and health policy.

"The nitwit doctor!" he spluttered. "The nefarious quack
claimed he found urine in my whisky!"

Poets rested from the world on Bundy Drive—Robert Hill-
yer, for one. Musicians, newspapermen, curators of museums,
and art dealers popped in and out or sometimes stayed for
a dinner prepared by Decker—but occasionally spoiled in the
pot when the host accidentally saw a sunset or thought of
his mother and took to the bottle too early in the evening.

But the most arresting personality of all who regularly
made of Decker's studio a clubhouse for bohemians was a
self-proclaimed genius, Sadakichi Hartmann. Old Sadakichi's
burst of coarse hair caused Jack Barrymore to describe him
as "the Gray Chrysanthemum." This skinny, prancing, cynical, yet beauty-loving wraith was half Japanese and half

German. He now was residing in a hut on an Indian reservation near Banning.

Barrymore and Decker, one jestful day in the late 1930s, said that I should write a story of this eerie Jack-of-all-arts. Journalists of the yon days had written much of Hartmann and with a variance of opinion, all the way from pronouncing him a startling cad to suspecting that he might sneak in one day as something of a prodigy.

I have referred to him in one of my books as "a bamboo bridge connecting the artistic and the literary scene of the 1880s with that of our own time." He looked like a forgotten potato and had the astringent wit of an unfrocked prior of the neo-Gothic age.

"You are a connoisseur of human oddities," Barrymore said to me. "Here is your chance to chronicle a living freak presumably sired by Mephistopheles out of Madame Butterfly."

I demurred on the ground that I already had my storyteller's eye upon a one-hundred-and-one-year-old mystic, Dr. Alexander J. McIvor-Tyndall, master of thought-transference, clairvoyance, and various other occult concerns. I had lodged the very tall and handsome centenarian at the Mark Twain Hotel, a convenient place for our interviews, and given him a walking stick with a gold band on it, engraved with praises of his esoteric skill. The cane pleased him, and the Mark Twain pleased him, partly because I picked up the tab and partly because the good doctor communicated on occasion with the spirit of the late Samuel Clemens, and even exchanged pleasantries with the shade of the great author—or so he said.

Barrymore objected to my choice of story material. "Your ancient table-rapper is apt to die on your hands at any moment and leave you with nothing better than a ouija board and the hotel bill. But Sadakichi"—he raised his eloquent hands heavenward—"his story would be a pilgrimage to the tomb of Sigmund Freud."

I rented a theater for a single performance, at which the six-foot-four-inch Dr. McIvor-Tyndall demonstrated his sorceries before an audience of some fifty persons, all deadheads. With a blindfold drawn over his bright blue eyes, he proceeded to discover pins hidden in the dusty stage draperies; to describe accurately the contents of purses, wallets, and coat pockets; to explore Adolf Hitler's mind—in absentia of course. Then, after the performance, he mislaid the gold-banded walking stick and lost his bifocals—and could not find these articles high or low. Well . . .

I conferred with Messrs. Decker and Barrymore that evening. "Gentlemen," I said, "I believe I shall undertake the story of your Sadakichi Hartmann after all. My aged warlock conked out on me."

The furtherance of this story will take shape as it may, and in the manner directed by the mood that springs, as if of its own accord, from notes set down at the scene by myself and others, in anticipation of these minutes of the last meetings of my good companions.

By a majority vote—Mr. Fields dissenting—we agreed to treat Sadakichi, both in person and in print, as an artistic hero of the first class. He in turn accepted our tongue-in-cheek deference as a well-merited recognition of his genius.

Before a year had passed we began to realize that our magnificent charlatan actually had been many things in many places. If anyone's frustrations, torments, impulsive actions, or stubborn show of courage in times of personal chaos had been more colorful than Sadakichi Hartmann's during his almost eighty years of life, none of us hitherto had met such a human paradox, except among the pages of Cervantes and Rabelais.

"But I say he is a no-good bum," Mr. Fields demurred again and again.

As an apprentice at a Munich theater, the young Sadakichi had spied upon the mad King Ludwig in the royal box during Wagnerian rehearsals. At a later day Sadakichi had been befriended, then denied, by Stéphane Mallarmé, the symbolist poet, in Paris, and by novelist Paul Heyse in Munich and again in Berlin. Sadakichi observed that Paul Verlaine had a habit of chewing his pencils; and when the poet died a pauper Sadakichi and Verlaine's bereft mistress chewed several dozen cheap pencils, which Hartmann then proceeded to sell as authentic mementos—thereby managing to pay the funeral expenses, with enough left over for refreshments.

The durable cadger stole a fan from the collection of Anatole France, tried to sell it back to the Gallic novelist, then bartered Monsieur France's letter of accusation to an autograph collector in exchange for a supper at Maxim's with a Montmartre femme and two bottles of Pol Roger.

Whistler conversed with Sadakichi briefly on the Paris boulevards, then sent him on his way. In 1910 Hartmann wrote a book about the artist, a work accounted by some critics as a revealing and judicious estimate of that painter's repertoire.

During his young manhood in Boston, Philadelphia, and New York, Sadakichi was lionized and denounced by turn; was thrown into jail for alleged blasphemous writings; saw both sides of the New England doors of Whittier and Emerson; and hopscotched up and down the eastern seaboard with the self-confidence of Puss-in-Boots, a celebrity one day and a pariah the next. He sought to gather roses but mostly got their thorns.

Gertrude Stein said of him, "Sadakichi is singular, never plural."

Sculptor Augustus Saint-Gaudens wrote to Hartmann in 1896, "What you think of matters of art I consider of high value."

"I still say he is a bum," declared W. C. Fields.

Hartmann in his time served as art critic in various Eastern cities, lectured on perfume, wrote five books, numerous poems and pamphlets, crowned himself King of Bohemia in the Greenwich Village of the 1890s and early 1900s; almost starved, sneered, and was sneered at; was wedded twice and engaged in an extramarital passage with a poetess toward the end of his first marriage. In all he sired thirteen children, to most of whom he gave the names of flowers or herbs. Now, old and dehydrated in Southern California, he was thought by federal officials to be an American Indian; but the government men were unsure of his totem or his tribe.

A dancing invalid for half his lifetime, Sadakichi said, "My ailments are exceeded only by my debts." Though asthmatic and deviled by a hernia, he could dance like a faun. His hands, long-fingered and suggesting animated pieces of cloisonné, were incapable of an ungraceful movement. He was almost six feet tall, weighed less than one hundred and forty pounds, mostly bone, and had a quick strength that amazed everyone, even those who had heard of his skill at Judo wrestling.

He fashioned a large truss for his hernia, and from necessity wore the cumbersome device in a way that emphasized his satyrlike appearance. During the Bunny-Hug vogue, the father of a debutante ordered our hero from the mansion when his attention was called to Sadakichi's Priapean contour as the spry guest danced with the heiress.

Upon hearing of this unjust ouster, and the cause of it, Barrymore rose from his velour-upholstered chair to bow to Sadakichi. "Sir, until now I have been known to the peanut munchers as 'the Great Profile.'" He bowed once more, like General Lee at Appomattox. "I now surrender the title to you, with all the honors—or lack of them—that go with it."

We who stayed up of nights at Decker's studio regarded Sadakichi as the most prodigious sack of sticks ever faggoted by the Almighty. We saw in him a cunning fellow who would lift your watch but whose critical integrity in matters of art was so fiercely constant that his opinions were not for sale. He acknowledged but one goddess, and her name was Beauty.

Barrymore and Decker volunteered to serve as my associates in the gathering of material for a book about this living gargoyle, a work Barrymore hoped would be "the most significant example of man's career among windmills since the time four centuries ago when Señor Miguel de Cervantes' tall and daffy jockey had a leg up on Rocinante."

Thus began the quest for Sadakichi, a task engendered in waggish minds. Yet the more we played at this game, the greater our interest became. I employed three successive secretaries to set down the words of the irascible critic; paid his hotel bills; gave him an overcoat, which he wore even in the hottest weather; and provided him with gallons of brandy and pecks of medicine for his asthma. For all these favors I received from him abuse, both written and oral; but I had good reason to believe that the old rascal had a hidden affection for me, as well as an unhidden one for my bankroll.

Again and again I began to write this book, only to have the events of wartime or my own personal affairs block the enterprise. On several occasions the adverse opinions of strong-voiced strangers dissuaded me. The bloodstreams of two international enemies ran in Sadakichi's veins, and whenever we are at military odds with other peoples of the earth, stories of aliens are about as welcome to us as the great pox.

Then on November 21, 1944, Sadakichi died in St. Petersburg, Florida, and I not only began to miss him, but also had to admit that the old wayfarer was the most unusual character I ever had met or hoped to meet this side of the nine moons of Saturn.

*Nothing has changed since
the dusk of the gods:
Drift of water, and ways of love.*
—Sadakichi

When in 1918 I began my newspaper time in New York, Sadakichi Hartmann had been absent for two years from the downtown inns. He was still well remembered, however, to the west and to the south of Washington Square —by some as a lunatic who lived off the cuff, and by others as the possessor of random talents as an art critic and evangelist of dissent.

The survivors of an unharnessed period in art, letters, and politics in Greenwich Village agreed that Sadakichi backed away from no one, and that he could get into trouble and out of it in the most amazing ways. The police saw in him a constant nuisance, one who made major disturbances of minor incidents. The Village patrolmen hesitated to take him in tow, for he could persuade even the municipal bench that New York's Finest were born without brains. He once stole a taxicab, and was acquitted in Jefferson Market Night

Court after he proved that he did not know how to drive a motor vehicle.

The courtroom gallery of poets and peasants rose en masse to shout, "Sadakichi is free!"

"I always *have* been!" their hero announced.

This vagabond scoffer not only believed that the world owed him a living, but proved his theory. He had a hundred cunning methods of winning entrance to a victim's house, and perhaps twice as many of staying on there. Although he would get into a benefactor's hair soon enough, as the saying is, he managed to defend his status as an unpaying guest with every ruse known to the mendicants of old. If given the boot—as was bound to happen eventually—he was likely to make a return visit on some pretext or other—such as having forgotten a manuscript or an article of wear.

One day long ago Henry Clay Frick asked him to leave his Fifth Avenue art annex for saying, "You are a great man in a small way." On his way out of Mr. Frick's then private gallery, Sadakichi convinced the butler that he had mislaid his upper dentures. He returned to the north wing, pretended to find his teeth near an ancient bust of Nero, then somehow placated Mr. Frick, who invited him to lunch. As the coffee was being served, the financier once again asked Sadakichi to get out—this time permanently— because of the remark, "America is a race of pyramid builders—building up to colossal failures. Former paupers think they are great men. You should tell all about this in a book about yourself, to be called 'The Tom Thumb of the Coke Ovens.' "

Amy Lowell in 1911 invited Sadakichi to inspect her collection of manuscripts. She became concerned when her guest charged that Keats didn't know a Grecian urn from a Pompeiian latrine.

"Sadakichi," she said, "you are the most mysterious man in American literature."

"And you," he replied, "are the greatest cigar smoker since General Grant."

When pianist Moriz Rosenthal, pupil of Liszt, executed a series of rapid scales while playing the "Hungarian Rhapsody" at a Carnegie Hall concert, Sadakichi made a megaphone of his long hands and shouted from his place in the gallery, "Is this necessary?"

While ushers led him toward the nearest exit Hartmann said, "I am a man needed but not wanted."

Not only was he ejected for cause from mansions, concert halls, studios, and saloons, but sometimes from a city. Early in this century St. Louis found him obnoxious, a threat to its civic pride. The city fathers at that time were completing plans for a world's fair to celebrate the centenary of the Louisiana Purchase. They invited Sadakichi to lecture on St. Louis art.

The lovers of culture bridled when their guest began his speech with, "Dirty! Dirty! Dirty! One, like Pontius Pilate, must continually wash his hands here. Your art is as feeble as your beer business is sturdy. St. Louis is the city of the dead *fleur-de-lis—*"

Strong citizens dragged Sadakichi from the platform. Next day the newspapers advised the critic to leave town at once, and a committee saw him to the railway station. There he made a farewell speech. "You pride yourselves on your clubs. Year in, year out, you chirp and twitter, loiter, buzz, and gabble about momentous nothings. The members keep the clubs exclusive, with no intent but to spin themselves, by endless strings of talk, into a cocoon of their own. St. Louis, *requiescat in pace!*"

Some years afterward anarchist Emma Goldman delivered a St. Louis lecture on "Misconceptions of Free Love." Sadakichi unexpectedly appeared on the platform to recite, as an afterpiece, his poem "Betrayed."

"What are you doing here?" a newspaper reporter asked Sadakichi.

"I am giving St. Louis another chance."

Unlike those star boarders who win free meals and lodgings by means of flattery, Sadakichi used insults and browbeat his hosts without ceasing. A Long Island millionaire once made the mistake of offering Sadakichi his country place for a weekend after the big house had been closed for the winter and the servants had left. It was beneath Sadakichi's dignity to recoal the basement furnace. He also ignored the woodpile, and for the sake of warmth knocked out the alternate balusters of an Edwardian stairway in the reception hall, which he placed as logs on the andirons. These, together with some magazines and newspapers, became fuel for several evenings at the hearth.

When the host learned of this atrocity he got in touch with the Nassau County constabulary, to charge Hartmann with arson and vandalism.

Sadakichi stayed out of that jurisdiction for the time being but said that the design of the stairway had been immeasurably enhanced and lightened because of the thinning-out process. Hartmann waited until the millionaire left for Europe, then went by train to Nassau County. He walked from the station to the country place and let himself in with a key he had had the foresight to keep. He first saw to it that all the shades were drawn and the shutters closed, then turned on every electric fixture in the house. He left a note: "Let there be light."

The electric bulbs burned all winter long.

Surprisingly enough, many women found Sadakichi a charming person, notwithstanding his leathery jaws and bamboo frame, his self-confessed Peeping-Tom tendencies, and the fact that he did not smell like Paris in the spring. As he became old his bloodshot eyes nested in wrinkled triangles—not almond-shaped eyes, as one might expect from his fraction of oriental descent—and the triangles became mere slits whenever he delivered a feline remark.

When speaking, which was much of the time, he would open his jaws until one had an oral surgeon's view of his throat; then he would spew an ironical "Hah!" as though to underscore the attack, or say, "Thank you very much." He never would say "Good-by," but instead used "Hello" as a word of farewell. More often than not it was difficult to understand what he was saying; but, oddly enough, whenever he read his own verses, or talked about himself, his enunciation became not only quite distinct but elocutionary in quality.

Sadakichi seldom spoke ill of a woman, and, in fact, praised not a few. He had greatly admired his sometime Boston neighbor Mary Baker Eddy, and referred to the religious philosopher as "Baker Eddy." He had an annoy-

ing way of shortening or changing entirely the names of
important persons of the past or present, a quirk exercised
by opinionated men, mostly authors; George Bernard Shaw,
for one. Hartmann was writing a drama in verse about Mrs.
Eddy when his own death intruded.

"She was a quiet, wonderfully attractive woman," Sadakichi said of Mrs. Eddy. "I believe she treated every human
being as if that person possessed deep and startling attributes. She was the greatest spiritual expression of the century."

Hartmann had held a platonic regard for Isadora Duncan,
with whom he had danced privately in Paris long ago. Another woman much admired by him, but at a later time, was
motion-picture actress Aileen Pringle, who had befriended
him. Perhaps the last woman to enjoy Sadakichi's complete
approval was Phyllis Decker, wife of John Decker. Hartmann's letters to Phyllis strongly indicate that he was not as
indifferent to a show of kindness as he constantly pretended.

"Why do women find this fugitive from an embalming
table so attractive?" I once asked John Barrymore.

"Because he looks like a sick cat," he replied. "Women are
nuts about sick cats."

Sadakichi went to California the first time (1916) for his
health; and the second time (1922) "out of despair." His
career in New York's Greenwich Village would seem second-
ary, I should think, in comparison to his many other "lives";
but he always spoke with a special show of relish of his
reign there as King of Bohemia.

Although New York soon forgets its darlings of yesterday,

the districts and the neighborhoods keep alive the memory
of certain former residents—especially of those zealots who
howled with hunger while awaiting an appointment with
Fame. Sadakichi had been a lively habitué of Greenwich Village before the time of the migration of sanctioned painters,
poets, and others of creative persuasion, uptown or to West-
chester County, or to the rural colonies of Connecticut and
Pennsylvania.

Late in 1918 the Village entered a postwar phase of mock-
art, pseudo-bohemianism, and mating without benefit of
banns. Several authentic artists, to be sure, mostly the old-
sters, stayed on, as did certain long-time occupants of the
Tenth Street Studio Building.

That weathered structure of Haverstraw brick had been
built in 1857 from designs by Richard Morris Hunt. It had
been the first New York structure exclusively occupied by
artists. Frederick Church, Stafford R. Clifford, Albert Bier-
stadt, William M. Chase, and John La Farge had been ten-
ants in the building, which has been described by painter
Hugo Ballin as "the navel of the artists of New York."

In his own young days Ballin frequently saw Hartmann
entering—or more likely being thrown out of—this and other
Village art centers. Ballin first met Sadakichi in 1902 or
1903, on a day when Hartmann was being kicked out of the
Grove Street studio of William J. Baer, the miniaturist.
Sadakichi had been free loading on Baer, and now was being
urged to go elsewhere, after he had composed a scurrilous
newspaper article against Baer's painter friend Robert Blum.

Blum had been Whistler's roommate in Venice. Sadakichi
hero-worshiped Whistler, perhaps because both men used

feline strategies when attacked. Hartmann reviled Blum for
having said that Whistler was "the most awful coward on
the face of the earth."

Ballin recollects that Hartmann (then thirty-eight or
thirty-nine years old) "always looked as if he only exhaled,
and never inhaled," and went on to say, "The last time I saw
him he was crossing Vine Street in Hollywood, with some
tired and worn sheets of paper under his arm that he'd fin-
gered for months, I suppose. He looked as if his head was
always anxious to get there before the rest of him."

During the post-World War I hurly-burly in New York
the name of any minor celebrity who left town to go to California usually became as neglected as an epitaph. Sadakichi's
name, however, was an exception. He often was spoken of
during a dinner at Luchow's, or at the Brevoort, the Lafay-
ette, or during a Prohibition gin-seminar at Barney Gallant's
or Romany Marie's.

Aside from this hearsay evidence of his past I had no
knowledge of the man. As to his California activities I stayed
in the dark, although actor Matt Moore reported that Hartmann was living in a shack at Beaumont and subsisting on a
diet of stolen potatoes.

Sadakichi, Moore said, had taught some children to filch
these potatoes at night from a field adjoining his Beaumont
hut. He trained the young poachers in the art of cleverly re-
placing the loam of the robbed patches. The farmer, puzzled by the poor yield of certain areas or by wilting foliage,
accused the local dealer in seed-tubers of selling him inferior
stock; and then reread the literature on virus disease, ring

wilt, fungus, mosaic, scab, blight, gophers, plant lice, and all other known enemies of the potato.

Hartmann returned to New York in 1922 to haunt the scenes of his Village heyday. By this time many of his old friends had gone to the cemetery and Sheridan Square was overrun with tourists. A season of escapades failed to bring him the kind of notoriety he once had enjoyed, so he quit the field and started out for California a second time, ill and embittered; but he stopped over at various cities on the way, to sponge upon art lovers in the provinces.

It was not until 1939, when I had left my summer home on Fire Island to go to the California studio of RKO, that I joined the long list of Sadakichi Hartmann's grubstakers. Unlike many of his rooked contributors, I enjoyed the experience.

My friend John Barrymore was in Chicago at this time, cavorting in that odd stage venture *My Dear Children.* In Hollywood, John Decker had not yet moved down to Bundy Drive; he was living in a hillside studio that once had been a sanitarium for tuberculosis sufferers, and managing to get along haphazardly on money earned by painting portraits, in comic imitation of the old masters, of Clark Gable, Beatrice Lillie, Harpo Marx, Fanny Brice, and many others.

The night before I called on him the artist had fractured his nose against the windshield of his car. He had driven his antique automobile into a concrete pillar at the fork of two roads, one of which led up a hill to his studio. "It's the third time I've broken my beak," he observed. "I'm getting to look more like Michelangelo every day."

He selected a letter from a pile of unpaid bills. It was

from Sadakichi Hartmann, postmarked Banning, California. Decker handed me the letter and said, "You promised Barrymore and me that you would get in touch with Sadakichi and do his story. He writes that you are missing your only chance to become famous. How about it?"

The next day I wrote to Sadakichi. In reply I received a telephone call from Banning (collect, of course). I could make out little that the man was saying. He muttered and spewed and cackled, coughed and wheezed. It sounded as though a kettle of macaroni had boiled over on the stove.

I did manage, however, to gather that he was a very great man and that he would come to see me at the studio—but expected me to send him five thousand dollars at once. He finally settled for twenty dollars, which I mailed to him that same afternoon.

In fact I was visiting my skeptical friend W. C. Fields at the time I made out the check, and borrowed an envelope and a postage stamp from him.

"I always shudder when I see you sign a check," the comedian said. "You are the perfect type for blackmail."

A newspaper reporter was interviewing Mr. Fields this day, and among other things had asked his views on sex.

"It is off the record, Mr. Fields," the reporter said. "I just want to know."

"On or off the record," said the red-nosed authority on almost any subject, "you can say this for me. There may be some things better than sex, and some things may be worse. But there is nothing exactly like it."

TWO

If we were able to tell
When old age would come our way,
We would lock the door, muffle the bell;
Tell him to come some other day.
                                        —Sadakichi

In the fall of 1939 I was working at the studio quarters of Leo McCarey. This master of screen comedy would have liked to be a writer of popular songs, but instead had to be reasonably content with his status as a world-famous director of films.

Several men of my acquaintance have had fierce ambitions to be songwriters instead of celebrities in their own familiar arenas; among them, New York's former mayor, James J. Walker, and the late Ring Lardner. McCarey, I thought, readily would have exchanged his screen classic, *Going My Way*, for a Tin-Pan Alley acceptance of his ditty "Tearbucket Jim."

"I had one song published," he confided once. "It was called 'When the Eagle Wraps Its Wings around the Kaiser. But it came out the very day of the Armistice. What irony!

Like the time mother entered me in a baby contest. There were sixteen candidates, and somehow I was seventeenth in the judging."

Leo played the piano well and would oblige at any time with a recital. Sometimes he would play all afternoon, a pastime that did not advance our picture work but made us feel better.

My room was an annex to McCarey's elaborate quarters and looked like a branch office of the public library—except that no books rested upon the shelves that lined the walls. Since I believed that books, or literature of any sort, were out of place in a picture studio, I wondered how I might enhance the appearance of the shelves. I sought the advice of W. C. Fields, whose masterpiece of interior decoration was his own living room. He had solved the problem of bare floor space by filling it with a pool table.

"First see to it that you have strong locks on every door," the great man said. "Then line the shelves with booze."

I was not drinking, but Fields' idea suggested a way to decorate my studio quarters. I sent out for two hundred bottles of a certain soft drink, and placed them on the shelves. My office took on the aspect of a nook at the Farmers Market.

To lessen the monotony of the soft-drink array I asked John Decker to paint for my office a picture of Mr. Fields as Queen Victoria. When I received the finished portrait in its authentic heavy gilt frame, I was delighted to look upon Fields' puffed cheeks, red nose, the Victorian fan in hand, the necklace and white bonnet. For good measure, the artist had placed in the background the strutting dandy so often

seen in the advertisements for Johnny Walker whisky. I
hung the portrait in the only vacant space on the wood-
paneled wall.

Actors and writers called all day long at my office to see
this picture. Decker scented a Hollywood renaissance and
began to paint and sell replicas of this portrait to all comers.
Soon my precious painting became known all over town as
a copy. I heard such patronizing comments as, "Oh, I saw
the original of this picture at Chasen's Restaurant"; or, "Sir
Cedric Hardwicke has the one this was copied from." I eventually grew weary of these slanders and gave the portrait as
a valentine to Uncle Claude—Mr. Fields' unpublicized middle name.

Upon his first glimpse of the portrait hanging among the
soft drinks Uncle Claude's whisky-tenor voice sounded a
protest. "Sabotage! Decker has kicked history in the groin."

He thumbed his ripe tomato of a nose and announced that
he must be on his way to see a friend who had got into a bit
of trouble. "The impulsive chappie," he explained, "is too
vain to wear glasses. Not long ago a lady in a bathing suit
struck his fancy. He did not know that the little chickadee
had just been paroled from a beauty clinic after a face-lift-
ing and reducing job, and mistook her for eighteen." Fields
turned at the door to utter one of his homilies. "Ah, how
often we stick out our chins and get hit on the button! Our
pal went to bed with Little Red Riding Hood and woke up
with her grandmother. Silly boy!"

After Uncle Claude had gone a studio policeman arrived
at my office. "There's a crazy guy out there at the old gate
yelling for Fowler. Keeps yelling like a maniac. All I can get

out of him is, 'Does a fellow named Fowler work here?'
When I told him he smelled of whisky he said I ought to be
smelling his genius. Should I call the prowl car?"

"No," I said. "Let Mr. Hartmann come on the lot."

"Oh, you *know* him?"

"I'll take care of him personally."

"He's at the old gate, yammering and pounding."

The studio policeman had reference to an iron-grilled
outer gate that had been locked for many years. No one now
used it or even had a key to it. I found Sadakichi standing
there at the wrong gate, as, in a broad sense, he had stood
so many times.

He scouted me with an air of disapproval. I could see John
Decker's portrait of him spring to life—the one now owned
by Burgess Meredith: the saffron hands, the wrinkled eye-
lids fluttering, the thin gray mustache on a long lip. Only he
seemed more threadbare than in the painting—a tattered
truant from an old men's home.

The California sun stood high this hot day of autumn, but
my visitor wore a seedy overcoat buttoned loosely about his
meatless ribs. His old fedora hat, with grease waves on the
cloth band, and a size too small, was perched upon a rick
of gray hair. Sadakichi's jaws worked constantly, whether or
not he was speaking; his loose false teeth made a clicking
sound, as of dice in a gambler's hand.

I reached through the grille of the old gate. "Sadakichi, I
am happy to know you."

"Is that remark a sample of your brilliance?"

"Would you please come to the main office on Gower?
This gate is closed."

"I want this gate," he said, and his long jaws chewed the words.

I attempted to explain. "It hasn't been opened in years."

"Is it the Holy Door of Saint Peter's?"

"If you will go to the main entrance," I said, "you will receive a princely reception. Maybe I'll hire an orchestra."

He grinned, and his face took on the appearance of a stale coffee cake with a crack in it. "You may omit the music."

I signed Sadakichi in at the reception desk, then showed him to my office a hundred yards or so distant on a studio street. Walking along, I thought that Hartmann looked like a stack of kindling with a weathered tarpaulin over it, animated by some black magic. He held his right arm straight down at his side and flexed his left arm behind his back, with the left hand clasping, behind the back, his upper right arm. Perhaps this posture relieved the pressure on his lungs, for he bubbled with asthma. At times his hips seemed to freeze his shank tops in the sockets and he would stop in his tracks; but as he set out again his stride was regular and his body nicely balanced.

"The cinema," he was saying, "is the scarlet woman of the arts. The studios will be closed one day and no one will miss them. Hollywood is the back porch of a dream."

Once inside my office Sadakichi squinted at the array of bottles, then at the Fields portrait, which he inspected at close range. "Hah!" he said. "Decker has been slumming again."

As he sat down his gray overcoat became unbuttoned as though of its own accord, to reveal a vest woven in a Wagnerian chorus of colors. I saw that his brown trousers were wrinkled and noticed the plaid socks and black congressional slippers which had insets of elastic webbing on the sides.

The outlines of the old man's frame showed through his medley of clothes. Until now he had appeared tall, though hunched over; but sitting opposite me his almost six feet of stature seemed to spend itself in the geometry of his bones.

He pushed the fedora hat back on his tumbleweed gray hair. "Where I come from," he announced, "and where I go doesn't matter. For I am Sadakichi Hartmann." He had a baritone voice that seemed to be caught in an eggbeater. "You may live a century, Fowler, but you will never meet another son of the gods like me."

McCarey happened to come in, but upon seeing my guest seemed to need a cup of strong black coffee. "Sorry," he said, turning to leave the room, "I didn't know you had opened a casting office."

Sadakichi ignored this interruption. He had his eyes on the bottles on the shelves. "You have something to drink?"

"As a matter of fact," I started out to apologize, "I'm not drinking, and—"

"What have your personal habits to do with my destiny?" he cut in. "Thank you very much."

"I hadn't expected a thirsty guest."

"You should always have something on hand to offset the stupidity of this place."

"Would you try one of these?" I indicated the vast supply. "I'll send out for ice."

He puckered his mouth until it resembled a dried prune with the stone removed. "What is this substance that you obviously are advertising?"

I named the trademark, then telephoned the commissary. After the ice arrived I opened a bottle and offered him a glass of the fizzing liquid. He smelled, then sipped it, quickly put it aside and made circles in the air with his long hands.

"From the kidneys of armadillos!" he exclaimed.

I put in a call to a friend on the lot to send over a bottle of Scotch. Later on, as Sadakichi liberally helped himself to the antidote, he said, "Be careful that you do not fall in love with your subject—in love with my wonderful character and genius. It will blind you, and your writing will suffer."

"From what I have heard," I said, "your life has been like an old paisley shawl, with many intricate designs, and here and there a moth hole."

"And Fowler crawling in and out of the holes," he replied. "Thank you very much."

"Tell me about yourself," I invited. "What do you think of yourself?"

"My whole make-up is mental. I am not capable of a pure emotion or a pure physical sensation. It is all drowned in mental considerations."

"Sadakichi," I inquired, "have you had many severe illnesses, other than a hernia and asthma?"

"Isn't that enough?"

From the McCarey suite came the sounds of "Tearbucket Jim." Sadakichi put aside a second whisky, rose from his praying-mantis position, and began a slow dance. He moved his hands and legs with rhythmic exactitude, grotesquely, but in arresting patterns of mobility.

"I am able to answer any query or express any sentiment by my gestures," he said as he moved to the music. "I prefer to dance in the desert. One day I shall landscape it, command waters to flow into it again, as in ancient times, and cause trees to grow; and then I shall have a stage that barely can match my genius in size and meaning and beauty."

A coughing fit caused him to leave off dancing. He shrugged, sat down, finished his drink. In spite of his eccentric manners, his Bowery-mission appearance, his ailments, and his chewed-up way of speaking, I saw in my scarecrow guest—or rather, I should say, felt—a warrior's spirit. No matter what the world might think of him he could not actually be a failure until he himself admitted it.

He wore his rags as though they were pieces of armor; and I sensed then, and later confirmed, that he possessed the heart of a champion.

My immediate friends of those days had this common denominator: strong hearts—in a physical as well as a symbolic interpretation of the phrase. It followed that they must die hard. They slugged it out with death, toe-to-toe, as is said of certain pugilists. Each man died hard, not only because of his passion for life, but because his heart had been the stoutest organ of a once-strong body. An artist should have the physical strength of a blacksmith: without it he will decline or perish before his time.

Barrymore would die, his insides burned out from going too near the flame, his liver shriveled to a small hard knob, and his kidneys almost gone; but the Viking's heart mocked the rest of him and kept him alive when it sometimes seemed that he could not live out the day. Decker would die when kidneys, liver, stomach, and all but the heart became mere remnants. So too, did the heart sustain, beyond all reasoned measure of survival, the powerful W. C. Fields, a man so perversely proud that he preferred to have men think him drunk when he actually was gravely ill.

Fields died on Christmas, a day he always had pretended to abhor. His doctors commented upon the regular pulsation of his heart when the rest of him had all but ceased to function. The defiant old artist fell away from this world with a leer for death, which he personified as the Man in the Bright Nightgown.

The self-destruction of these physically powerful men—and each of them, their doctors said, had the attributes of longevity—supplies a valid argument for temperance, as well as for other kinds of moral restraint. Notwithstanding their shortcomings—their lack of self-discipline among other things—the members of this group acted valiantly in times of adversity. They blamed no one but themselves for the outcome of their follies; self-pity was a stranger to them. They paid all penalties without welshing and lived their last hours without cringing.

I saw in the fierce old bundle of sticks that was Sadakichi Hartmann a man of courage. At that moment he ceased being a stranger to me.

So eager to live!
How patiently you watched
For the first fair day.
Rain-mists still blurring the way
Now also will clear away.
                    —Sadakichi

In November I went with Leo McCarey to his mountain lodge near Big Bear Lake. The colony of summer residents had gone, and no piano and no Sadakichi interrupted
our work.

After ten days we set out on the return journey to town,
with Leo singing happily at the wheel of his car. The sun
disappeared as abruptly as a Hollywood friend, and Leo
turned on the headlights. We were traveling at the rate of
ninety-five miles an hour. The four-lane highway seemed
clear of traffic until an elderly motorist in a big automobile
quite unexpectedly emerged from an orange-grove trail to
our left. He started to turn into our lane. The hammers of
hell began to pound, and the lights went out.

I afterward learned that McCarey was hurled one hundred and twenty-six feet—by police measurement—into the

freshly irrigated orange trees. The car, with me folded inside it, turned over three times. I stayed pinned upside down for half an hour, my clothes and body drenched with raw gasoline. I suffered two split vertebrae, three cracked ribs, a skull injury, and wrenched knees. Otherwise I was as good as new.

An ambulance arrived in the darkness to take the unconscious McCarey to the nearest hospital at Covina. The ambulance doctor had been unable to find my pulse and understandably had sent for a mortician.

I briefly came to in the hearse. "Is anyone here?" I called out.

A voice seemingly from far away answered me. I remember little that it said, except for the announcement that the owner of the voice was not a physician and was not equipped with sedatives.

Although I had no recollection of the preceding events, it occurred to me that I had been in some action more strenuous than a fistfight. No siren was sounding, nor was the vehicle in a race with time. The voice quite suddenly became clearer, and with it another sound, like that of a piece of wicker furniture when someone stirs upon its seat.

As a police reporter I had been familiar with coroners' baskets, but until now never had demonstrated one. I passed out, but not on—as expectant relatives say of a more or less dear one just before the will is read.

At the hospital next day Fields persuaded a nurse to tell me not to let the doctors apply casts, bandages, or splints. He disliked all members of the medical profession, some of whom had sued him for the non-payment of bills. Injustice of any sort offended this self-appointed champion of human rights.

"You will come out looking like a pretzel," the nurse said, relaying Fields' message, "if you let those croakers put their contraptions on you. I'll send over some rum—man's best friend."

As a warning against bone doctors Fields frequently would recite his own hospital experience with a broken neck, a mishap that had occurred in an automobile accident. He had permitted no protective cast or collar to be placed on his cracked head-rest. Instead he lay immobile for weeks until the neck bones knitted.

To celebrate the healing, and with his chin by necessity still held high, Uncle Claude got out of his hospital bed, a martini in his hand, and shuffled into the corridor. There he stumbled against a wheelchair and fell to the floor, with outcries against the inventor as well as the manufacturers of wheelchairs and promises to sue everyone connected with the hospital, including the Sisters of Mercy. His newly mended neck miraculously held together, but his tail bone, or coccyx, snapped.

"Damn it all!" he roared as attendants helped him to his feet. "I came here with my top end busted and now my hind end's ruined. Worse still, I've lost my drink!"

I followed Uncle Claude's advice, dispensed with bandages and supports, and came out of the hospital in a miser's crouch. For a long time I had to use a cane; and even now, as I get out of bed, I sound like a castanet solo.

During my convalescence I forgot to get in touch with Sadakichi Hartmann. He sent word from Banning that I de-

liberately had planned this accident to escape doing his biography.

"Fowler is using this illness as an excuse to avoid becoming famous," he wrote Decker. "He suddenly realizes that I
am much too big a subject for his limited talents."

Hartmann's spleen again boiled over when McCarey, soon
after he left the hospital in May of 1940 (after a series of
nerve-splicing operations and with one arm still in a cast),
chartered an airplane to fly Miss Irene Dunne and several
other members of his troupe to Louisville, Kentucky, and
invited me to be his guest, to preview a picture made by him
prior to the automobile accident. The McCarey party would
attend the Kentucky Derby as well as the première of the
film.

Sadakichi denounced me for interrupting his biography
to go on a junket. The least I could do, he said, was to take
him to Louisville. When he found out later that I had invited an enthusiastic horse-player, the celebrated short-story
writer Frank Condon, to go along, Hartmann spluttered like
a defective radio set.

Condon was dying of cancer, and the journey to Louisville
would remain a bright memory during the few months left
to him. He won seventy-two dollars and forty cents on
Gallahadion, the long-shot winner of the race; and the be-
loved dean of sportswriters, Grantland Rice, gave him a
handsome overcoat, which he draped across a chair in the
bedroom of his Beverly Hills home and looked at every day.

"It will be just the thing to wear on chilly afternoons at
Santa Anita," he said a few hours before he died.

On Derby Day, as we were motoring from Churchill

Downs to our hotel, the McCarey car stalled near the Sea-
grams Distillery. We got out to stand at attention in honor
of our absent friend W. C. Fields.

"When Uncle Claude leaves us," said McCarey reverently,
"this place is bound to go out of business."

Upon my return to California I got in touch with Sadakichi. I promised to pay more attention to his genius and
sent him three hundred dollars, together with an invitation
to come to town for a housewarming at John Decker's Bundy
Drive studio.

By this time John Barrymore had returned to California,
confused and ill and beset by domestic issues. He was reaching the end of his fourth marriage at his Bellagio Road home
in Bel-Air, and, as we now know, the end of his tempes-
tuous life as well.

Our group met during the next four years or so at Decker's
studio. During many days and nights of two of those memor-
able years, Barrymore would gaze upon the artist and his
easel and seem to be reliving his own early ambitions to be
a painter.

The Bundy Drive studio in Brentwood was a cottage of
rural English design. Some artists might have found the
brown-beamed room in which Decker painted unsuitable for
their work. One side-window caught merely a fraction of the
north light—what with the scant dimensions of that window
and the shadows cast by trees near the house.

"To hell with north light!" Decker said. "My pictures are
meant to be hung in the light of electric lamps; so I create
them in that kind of light."

The first things Decker painted for the housewarming were the panels of his front door. He put upon the door a coat of arms, possibly his father's, and improvised a motto: "Useless, Insignificant, Poetic."

Next he fashioned a mailbox, inexpertly carpentered from odds and ends of board but beautifully decorated with window boxes and gay flowers. Most of the mail delivered to this box consisted of overdue bills, but now and again there would come good news, as the time Decker was notified that he had won the John Barton Payne medal at the Virginia Museum of Fine Arts for his painting "The Strong Man."

This was one of a series created by Decker during his "Clown Period." He sold the prize-winning picture for a thousand dollars to Frank Cavett, co-author of the screenplay *Going My Way*. Soon thereafter Decker borrowed the painting for a one-man show, and, without asking Cavett's permission, sold it off the gallery wall for twenty-five hundred dollars to songwriter Jimmy McHugh. The artist gave Cavett back his thousand dollars and then scattered his own profits among the Sunset Strip cafés.

Oddly enough, Decker's ways of juggling art deals did not alienate his friends. I soon enough learned not to submit my own Decker paintings for gallery display. He had once sold me an excellent still-life of zinnias, done with the palette knife, then resold it at his very next exhibition. Again, when I had allowed him to take home a blue-flower painting to give it a protective coat of varnish, I managed to rescue it as he was about to resell it to W. C. Fields.

Amid cries of "Snooping bastard!" by Uncle Claude and, "I thought you wouldn't mind if I made a buck," on Decker's part, I gave the artist the difference between the price I had paid and the amount Fields bid for the work. Both the artist and the comedian had roguish natures; but anyone who stayed mad at them would have been a serious-minded dullard.

To set down a guest list of the housewarming at the Bundy Drive studio would be a name-dropping exercise. Sadakichi was there, of course, and this is enough for the moment, especially since he denounced everyone, including Barrymore, and almost stank us out with a medicated pipe he puffed to alleviate his asthma.

In an aside to me Jack Barrymore said, "Can't you give him a cigar, or even a roman candle, instead of that vile calumet?" Then he smiled. "But I'm glad you've exhumed the old fellow. He's the last of the Pharaohs, and nicely mummified at that."

At this time Sadakichi had lodgings in a Wilcox Street hotel in Hollywood, at my expense, and I supplied him daily with imported beer and Cordon Bleu brandy. I also persuaded Dr. Samuel Hirshfeld to examine him and prescribe remedies for his asthma or for other ailments he might find.

"This old man should be operated upon for his hernia," the doctor advised. "He will not let me inspect the region of the lesion, but it is plain enough that it should be relieved surgically."

Sadakichi resented this proposal, especially since his procreative glands must be excised to reach the area of the rupture. "There will be no charge," said Dr. Hirshfeld.

Decker urged Sadakichi to say farewell to the glands. "They have served their purpose," he said, "and undoubtedly merit an honorable retirement."

"Ghouls!" cried Sadakichi. "No one will snatch my glands!" He turned his rage upon the doctor. "Why don't you men of medicine do something worth while instead of castrating a genius?"

Decker said that Sadakichi was behaving foolishly and recommended that Barrymore act as referee. When he spoke to Jack about this he tactfully withheld the name of the doctor. Hirshfeld had been Barrymore's physician during the period of his marriage to Dolores Costello, but because of a mistaken belief that the doctor wished to place him in a mental institution Jack had summarily crossed the family physician off his list. So, whenever I asked Dr. Hirshfeld to call upon Hartmann, I first saw to it that Barrymore was not likely to be present.

Barrymore sustained Hartmann's objection to the operation. "After all," said he, "it is hard to cast aside comrades of happier times."

"Other people," said Sadakichi, "talk and talk about dying. I'm *doing* it!"

After Sadakichi had vetoed the surgery I introduced him to his first secretary. At the outset that young woman seemed skeptical of recording his philosophies and self-praises, but soon found her work fascinating and eventually declared that Mr. Hartmann was a gentleman.

The hotel people held quite an opposite view. For one thing, Hartmann's kidneys were unpredictable; the cushions of the overstuffed chairs of his suite took on faded patterns and altered shades. Then, too, there was the evil-smelling pipe.

Sadakichi smoked a concoction of tobacco and the dried leaves of *Datura stramonium*, a shrub known to the ancients of India as poisonous, but which seemed to the residents of his hotel, and I quote, "Awful! At first we thought it was smog. Unless you make that stinking old bastard quit smoking it around here, we'll leave."

Our biographical interest in Sadakichi seemed to stimulate him. I promised him a thousand dollars but took the precaution of paying our ersatz hero at the rate of one hundred dollars a week. He had a long record, as the ever-dissenting Fields pointed out, of "taking the money and running for the train." Fields thought we were crazier than Sadakichi to waste either money or ink upon him.

"He's a skinny thief!" Uncle Claude exclaimed one day when John Decker's new watch disappeared. "I know a thief when I see one. When I was young I was the biggest thief at large. I'd steal golf balls, piggy banks of dear little kiddies, or nozzles off the hoses of the rectory lawn—anything and everything. Then, when I got into the chips myself and had plenty of dough, my character changed. From then on there was nothing I hated worse than a thief."

Matt Moore not long ago recalled an example of Sadakichi's hit-and-run activities. Hartmann had planned a double killing, with victims of no less celebrity and wealth than Charlie Chaplin and Douglas Fairbanks, Sr.

It was during the silent-film days when Chaplin fell in love, as it were, with Hartmann's genius. For a time they were inseparable—until Hartmann offended two outstanding elements of the Chaplin composite: the love of money and the love of self.

Chaplin never was known as Lord Bountiful. In less than a week of their association Hartmann discerned that not even he, the master moocher, could break the seal of the comedian's wallet. He decided to do the next best thing: he would ask Chaplin to introduce him to Douglas Fairbanks, Sr.

The athletic Fairbanks, early in 1924, was preparing *The Thief of Bagdad* for the screen. He was a direct sort of fellow, one who in his younger years had chosen Theodore Roosevelt as his model for strenuous actions and quick decisions. Upon meeting Sadakichi he cried out, "Bully! I want you to be the court magician in my next picture!" He turned to Chaplin. "Congratulate us both, Charlie."

Chaplin had just come from the dressing-room shower and wore an over-long Turkish towel. He happened to see himself in the mirror, became enchanted with the image, then rearranged the towel to simulate a Roman toga. He began to strut, as if on his way to the Forum. This pantomime was wasted on Sadakichi; his wits probably were concentrated upon how much salary he might wangle from Fairbanks.

Chaplin struck a senatorial posture. "Sadakichi, what role would you say I am playing?"

"Caesar's secretary," replied Hartmann.

Chaplin gave orders to bar the gate thenceforward against Sadakichi and urged Fairbanks not to hire him. But Fairbanks thought otherwise. He even agreed to pay his new actor two hundred and fifty dollars a week in cash and to deliver a case of whisky to his door every week during the next two months.

As the court magician, it was necessary for Hartmann to wear a glass-and-metal headdress, which weighed fifteen pounds. He actually felt ill much of the time on the set, for he had to stand for twenty minutes or so while the scene was properly lighted and the camera angles were selected, before rehearsing and finally playing the scene. He grew cross and frustrated.

Halfway through the picture he threatened to quit. If Hartmann were to walk out Fairbanks would lose heavily in terms of time and money spent on matter already photographed; all the scenes in which the court magician appeared would have to be scrapped and reshot. Fairbanks raised Sadakichi's salary; then for good measure provided a man of Hartmann's physique to pose in his place whenever the director and cameraman were readying the pertinent scene. Matt Moore believes this to have been the first time a stand-in was used.

Everything went smoothly for another week, and Fairbanks boasted that he had discovered one of the great character actors of all time.

One afternoon Sadakichi drew his pay, waited until the regular case of whisky arrived at his door, then went to San Francisco, there to hide in Chinatown. This desertion cost Fairbanks two hundred and fifty thousand dollars in production money; delayed the shooting of the picture; necessitated story changes, the restoration of certain sets and the rebuilding of others; and, for a time, soured the disposition of a most generous picture star.

When asked why he had victimized Fairbanks, Sadakichi merely waved a hand and said, "He tried to poison me with inferior whisky. Thank you very much."

CHAPTER

FOUR

A woman's death created me.
Rest with my thanks,
Rest softly under the hills
*   of Kobe;*
While wind and birds sing everlasting
Funeral rites to thee, my mother.
                                    —Sadakichi

W. C. Fields named it "Black Tuesday," the day our party called on him at his run-down estate on De Mille Drive in the Los Feliz district north of Hollywood. The property had stayed run down for the very reason that Uncle Claude was having a feud with his landlord.

Fields had leased the large house and extensive grounds when almost everyone but he was in a sorry cash position; then, when conditions improved, the landlord could not persuade his tenant to amend the terms of the long-term lease. He also had to supply gardeners, while W. C. gloated. Fields always knew his rights, even when he was wrong, and would not budge once he had made up his mind to resist man or beast.

"All landlords should get the electric chair," he said.

The landlord had made several reasonable suggestions of compromise and had offered to renovate the property if his tenant would see the light. "Not one cent for tribute," was the Fields reply. "Let the joint fall apart."

As a consequence of this deadlock the mansion took on the appearance of the House of Usher. Where the wallpaper had not fallen off, it hung like the tattered battle standards of Napoleonic campaigns. When the ground jiggled, as sometimes happens in California, plaster flecked the pool table in the drawing room. The warp of the carpets showed through at the three bars installed by the tenant. (He also had a portable bar for outdoor use or for any thirsty emergency in the hallways; another bar in the automobile trailer in which we used to travel to weekly prizefights at Jim Jeffries' barn; and a refrigerated chest bolted to the rear floorboards of his limousine and covered with a Mexican serape.)

Nasty-tempered as he may have seemed to strangers, particularly autograph-seekers, politicians, or landlords, Fields in private life was a most amiable host. If, as some persons assumed, Fields and his companions appeared unduly careless of public sanction of their ways, it should be remembered that all these men were on their last legs—and knew it. They had no time for simulated pleasantries, nor with the exception of Decker, who liked publicity, did they care what the newspapers might say of them.

They actually did not belong to this century, for all had been born before its coming. In effect they were misfits, whatever their fame, and unable to conform to an age of regimentation that, for good or ill, marked the rise of science and the decline of art. Each member of this group had known tragedy and pain, but elected to wear the mask of comedy for the world to see, if not to applaud.

The cronies who called upon Fields that Tuesday included Barrymore, Decker, Sadakichi, and myself. Uncle Claude greeted us in his second-floor "office." He looked like a Frans Hals burgomaster, well fed and gouty, as he sat behind the huge desk at which he was accustomed to stay for hours composing letters of denunciation to almost anyone.

He had on a white bathrobe of toweling material, in one pocket of which he kept perhaps thirty keys on a chain, and in the other a fat roll of currency. Whenever he stirred he sounded like the Prisoner of Chillon. Fields had extra locks on every chest-lid as well as on the doors of the various storerooms in the big house. He kept cases of liquor and beer behind these barriers; for, as he phrased it, even the one or two honest men now alive would not hesitate to steal when thirsty.

"What is your pleasure, gentlemen?" he asked, but before we could reply, said, "As if I didn't know!" He snapped on the switch of an intercom box, one of the many electrical gadgets on his crowded desk, and shouted into it, "Bring up some ice!"

With an "Excuse me for the nonce," Fields picked up a pair of large-size binoculars from the desk and went over to the window. He trained the lenses on the slopes of his lawn. "Those damned pelicans had better lay off my fish pond!" he said. "Why do these criminal birds have to put the bite on me?"

Gulls oftentimes swooped in from the Pacific to snatch

goldfish from the Fields lily-pond. He mistook them for pelicans and would blaze away at them with a heavy pistol that surely had belonged to one of General Phil Sheridan's lieutenants.

Fields now pointed his binoculars toward the road that lay beyond his acres and fixed the glasses on an automobile passing by. "Look!" he snarled. "Just look at him sailing past in that big car!" He turned from the window and on his way back to the desk explained, "Cecil B. De Mille goes up and down this road like he was the king-emperor. Just because the pike is named for him he thinks he owns it." Then he rasped into the intercom, "Damn it all! Where's the ice? I asked you to get it a week ago!"

He now lectured us at great length and loudly on the treachery of servants, alleging the unmarried state of their parents, and went on to say that if it were not for his stout locks, his pistol, and the fact that he could smell thieves a mile off, he would today be a poor man, rooked beyond all mercy or conscience. He patted the bulge made by his bankroll. "Everyone is on the make, and you're liable to be stuck up in your own boudoir. But they won't catch me off base! No sir! I keep this getaway money on my person at all times. You never can tell when Roosevelt will get another of his whims and close the banks."

The ice never arrived. It seems that Fields had neglected to turn off the switch of his intercom system while he was preaching against servants. They obviously had heard his indictments and felt a bit unwelcome. At any rate, they had packed up and left in a body.

Strikes of servants were not an uncommon event in the household of W. C. "It's capital *versus* labor all the time," he complained. "I've got to write to Westbrook Pegler."

During this scene Sadakichi had helped himself liberally from a bottle on the bar. "You've already made seven trips to the bar," Fields admonished him.

"Isn't that what it's for?" Sadakichi said.

"Why do you start drinking it all at once, and so early?" Fields asked. "Are you anemic?"

Sadakichi replied, "It gives me courage to meet the hardships of the day."

"Then you've got plenty of courage," said our host. He now confided to Barrymore, "I'm practicing self-restraint these days, Jack. I only drink half a pint before breakfast, and I've quit whisky entirely. Martinis are the thing."

"Uncle Claude," Decker said, "I understand the FBI is looking for you."

The great man paled—that is, all of his face paled except the broken veins over his cheekbones and the thousand-watt nose. "Where did you hear that?"

"You told me so yourself," said Decker. "This morning. Over the telephone."

Fields turned to Barrymore. "My memory is getting worse than yours."

John Barrymore's memory for recent events had become quite unreliable. On the motion-picture set he found it necessary to read the dialogue of the moment, written upon a slate held by a prompter off-scene. He called this slate his "idiot board," a descriptive phrase still used by studio crews.

Fields had just such a slate fastened to the wall of his upstairs study. He chalked daily reminders upon it, together with an occasional whimsy—such as this note addressed to his rosebushes: "Bloom, you bastards! Bloom!"

"It is part of my philosophy," W. C. finally said to Decker, "never to discuss matters of state with a commoner."

Sadakichi had fallen asleep in a barber's chair in an alcove adjoining the office. As explained by Robert Lewis Taylor in his excellent book on Fields, Uncle Claude used this chair to doze in when insomnia bothered him. He also would take catnaps out of doors beneath a canopy in the garden, while a servant sprayed a hose on the canvas shelter to simulate rain.

Fields cocked an ear as Sadakichi's snores began to outdo our conversation. He turned his small blue eyes toward me with a look of accusation. "Are you on the level about writing the life of this guy Hoochie-Kootchie?"

I nodded. "We are now gathering data about his birth and early life."

Our host thought this over for a time, then quite suddenly picked up a rubber toy made in the form of a claw-hammer and began to pound his desk with it. This was the same "hammer" a lady once described in court as the weapon W. C. had used upon her person in a moment of pique.

"Get him out of here!" The rubber hammer thumped again. "If the FBI finds this German-Jap on my hands I'll get life!"

We roused Sadakichi to take him to the hotel. As our car drew up at the curb on Wilcox Street, Barrymore said,

"When your sleepy Samurai awakens fully, find out *if* he was born, and *why*."

Sadakichi muttered something in German to Decker.

"What is Admiral Togo saying?" asked Jack.

"He wants to know if you're a Democrat or a Republican," said Decker.

"I'm a royalist," Barrymore replied.

When Sadakichi and I settled down in his suite he told me he had been born in Nagasaki, Japan, in the 1860s. His habit was to pare off a year or so as he grew older; but in a letter to Barrymore in 1929, offering his services as a press agent, Hartmann stated that he had been born in the year of the Battle of the Wilderness. That would have been in 1864, when General Grant was commander-in-chief of the Union Army. What his birth in far-off Japan had to do with the battle I could not imagine—unless it reminded him of the wilderness of his own affairs.

Sadakichi's Japanese mother, said he, married Otto von Hartmann when that roving gentleman had an assignment in Japan as an agent for the family's company of coffee importers. According to Sadakichi, the Hartmann family had owned and managed one of the largest coffee concerns in Hamburg, Germany, and had possessed considerable wealth.

Sadakichi had a brother Taru, who was two years older than he. At the time of Taru's birth the Japanese grandparents disowned their daughter for having married a foreigner. She died soon after Sadakichi's birth.

"I once had an inscribed wooden tablet," said Sadakichi, "which for a long time I mistook for a passport to identify oneself at the city gates at night, but which was an *inhai*, a memory tablet. My father once showed me a sheet of fibrous, half-transparent Japanese paper, scrawled all over with characters unintelligible to me, as proof of my existence."

During his mother's pregnancy, Sadakichi had been told, she had made daily pilgrimages to the temple, passing the stone lanterns and climbing the stone steps to pray near a bronze horse or to gaze out upon the harbor below the temple garden.

As his mother lay dying, Sadakichi went on to say, she asked Otto to take their infant children to Germany for a Western education. The elder Hartmann named his second boy Carl. Sadakichi's mother, he said, had given him his Japanese name, and explained that "*sada*" meant "virtue," and "*kichi*" meant "good fortune."

Professor Ashikaga of the University of Southern California at Los Angeles informs me that Sadakichi is a given name that means "steady luck." Evidently Sadakichi's mother was not clairvoyant—unless she meant steady bad luck.

"The moniker means 'Gimme some dough,'" said Fields.

"Gentlemen," said Barrymore, "Sadakichi is the mating call of rabid, though sacred monkeys, playing among the acorn towers of Angkor Wat."

Sadakichi's mother was denied burial in Nagasaki's hill cemetery. "Her body was cremated in Kobe," he said, "where the Kutobiki waterfalls spray the mountain slope. Her relatives, still scandalized by her marriage to an Occidental, strewed her ashes along the dusty road for donkeys to walk over."

Sadakichi's father took his two young sons to Hamburg. There he left them in the charge of his brother, Ernst Hartmann, and sailed away to the Fiji Islands. Sadakichi's earliest recollections were of smashing a glazed porcelain doll's head; and, later on, of the counting of the droppings of a pet rabbit. He also tried to bury alive one of his playmates.

"Such sweet goings-on," Jack Barrymore observed, "explain clearly why he grew up to be a critic. Sounds like Alex Woollcott."

Sadakichi recalled that upon several occasions he had peeked at the *Fräuleins* of the household staff as they undressed themselves. He calmly admitted doing this sort of thing in after years whenever he had the opportunity. "I was a student of anatomy," he said.

A year after the Hartmann boys' arrival at Hamburg, Sadakichi's father returned briefly, to marry a Hamburg woman who had enchanted him with her playing of the mandolin. Sadakichi's father and stepmother then went off to some faraway island in the tropics on their honeymoon.

Although Uncle Ernst continued to pay for the support of the half-caste children of Otto's first marriage, he found it expedient to ask his mother to manage their education. Grandmother Hartmann resided in Ernst's large house, the rooms of which contained many books and numerous art treasures.

Taru had asthma at this time. A physician prescribed for him the inhalation of burning paper impregnated with saltpeter, and also recommended the smoking of stramonium leaves.

"So that's where Sadakichi discovered the rancid substance!" was Barrymore's comment. "I thought he found it in Satan's snuffbox."

"When my brother woke me up at night with his asthmatic noises," Sadakichi told me, "I could not fall asleep again and, little wretch that I was, would mimic his pains. My mimicry one day became so real to me that I too was stricken with asthma, permanently."

The boys had private tutors. Sadakichi read much, learned English, was kissed when he was twelve, but preferred peeking at the *Fräuleins* to embracing them.

"My daydreams," he said, "excel all reality."

Sadakichi smoked his uncle's cigars on the sly and raided the wine cellar. He attended the theater frequently, as well as the opera, and fell in love with Wagner's swan-boat fantasies.

The family once made a Rhine journey. Sadakichi shot off firecrackers in the lobby of a hotel in Cologne, so it was decided to enter him as a cadet in the naval school at Kiel for discipline. His classmates taunted him for his Japanese ancestry, an experience that may have had much to do with his subsequent acidulous views of mankind and his seeming obsession to make the world pay a stud fee, retroactively, for his father's Japanese interlude.

At about this time the elder Hartmann returned from a tropical shore to arrange for his younger boy to go to America. The father and son traveled to Paris, then to Le Havre— the parent in a first-class, and the son in a third-class, railway carriage. To Sadakichi's pained surprise his parent gave him but three dollars and left him aboard the steamship *Lessing* bound for Hoboken, a voyage of fourteen days.

"The experience will give you character and resourcefulness," counseled the father. "You must learn to shift for yourself."

In speaking of this Sadakichi observed, "It was surely not an act of kindness to send a boy alone and almost penniless to a foreign land across the sea. My father did not even pay for the passage; he took the money out of my savings bank, in which I had hoarded some three hundred marks. Nor was it excusable that, while I was starving in Philadelphia, and when for half a year my father held a high position in New York, he never informed me of his presence. Events like these are not apt to foster filial piety."

With a knapsack on his back and a staff in his hand, Sadakichi set out on foot for Philadelphia. Occasionally he would get a lift in a wagon or cart. He had relatives in Philadelphia, but they were not overjoyed to see him at their door.

Sadakichi was about to tell me of his meetings with Walt Whitman, who had lived across the Delaware River in Camden, New Jersey, when the telephone rang. It was John Decker. He reported that our friend Barrymore had suffered a gastric upheaval. Doctors were endeavoring to make it possible for him to begin a motion picture next day at the Twentieth Century-Fox Studio.

Sadakichi made much of the fact that I regarded the health of a friend as more important than the biography of a genius. "The Muse will not like this, and neither will I, Fowler."

The next afternoon I received word that Barrymore would be able to work. Soon after this Fields telephoned to ask me, "How's the Monster?" He was not referring to Sadakichi but to Barrymore. Our nickname for Jack was "the Monster."

"Jack is going to be all right," I told W. C. "But the doctors have taken away his bottle."

"A lot of goddam sadists!" Fields exclaimed. "They deny a man his true nourishment, then ply him with tons of poisonous minerals instead." There was a pause, and I heard a gurgling sound, as of a mountain creek rippling over stones, then the smacking of lips. Fields then announced, "I've got good news—for a change. Yesterday," he went on to say, "was Black Tuesday. Remember? Well, today, my dear lad, is Vindication Wednesday. But suppose you and Decker come over to hear the story from my own lips."

Decker and I called upon the now-beaming Mr. Fields. The comedian was staying at home much of the time these days, for his once-sturdy legs were growing unstable—although I never knew him to stagger because of too much drink. His short excursions to Bundy Drive or to my house or to Gregory LaCava's place at Malibu or to his favorite restaurants summed up his travel, except for one long trip to Tijuana, Mexico, not long before he died. He had arthritis, among other ailments, and his small shapely hands had become incapable of performing the juggling tricks that had given him his early fame.

Our red-nosed chum was in wonderful humor, as compared to his low state of yesterday. He had persuaded his servants to call off their strike, and to demonstrate the way things stood he turned on the intercom and delivered a eulogy on the loyalty of his employees, their great love of him, and the certainty of their legitimate parentage.

He turned off the switch, then tested it carefully to see that it was not carrying his voice. Winking, like a sly troll, he whispered hoarsely, "They're a lot of no-good bastards! Lard-heads! Fiends! They think my nose is the red badge of cowardice. Eat me out of house and home, and besides that probably do the most awful things to my soup!"

"You telephoned that you had some news," Decker interposed.

"Oh yes. Yes. Even so." Fields once again tested the intercom, and lowered his voice as an added precaution. "It was about those miniatures you painted for me."

"I don't follow you," said Decker.

Some time before, Decker had painted three small ovals, caricature studies of a Washington woman whom Fields passionately disliked. He had no logical reason whatsoever for this animus, but then he seldom needed a logical reason to turn against anybody, and without notice.

Decker had given these small pictures to Fields. When held upside down they became grotesque anatomical views. "The FBI man wanted to see 'em," W. C. said. "Someone had blown the whistle on me."

Decker's mouth flew open. "Good Lord! *I* don't want to go to the can for painting them!"

Fields smiled condescendingly. "My boy, no one is going to land in the iron pavilion at Alcatraz. Be of good cheer."

W. C. explained that when the government agent had called by appointment, he had waited nervously for a hint that might reveal the purpose of the visit. Fields had expected the worst (as he always did when interviewed by a stranger), and with sound reason. The artful comedian frequently had gone to court to resist claims of all sorts made by his "Uncle Whiskers," as on the day when cross-examiners for the government asked him to justify, if possible, a tax deduction of twenty-five thousand dollars.

He said, under oath, that he had spent that preposterous amount upon gentlemen of the press.

"For liquor?" he was asked.

"No!" he shouted. "For milk!"

Need it be said that Mr. Fields lost his case? And was fined?

The FBI man, Fields told us, had seemed quite cordial this Wednesday morning. A courteous approach by a government sleuth was bound to stir Fields' anxieties. He had listened for the jingle of handcuffs.

"I understand," the official said to him, "that you own some interesting paintings, eh?"

Fields sparred with, "Oh no, no! I wouldn't say that! Just a lithograph of the Corbett-Sullivan fight, a photograph of Miss Mae West, and a few knickknacks here and there."

His visitor persisted. "No ladies' pictures?"

"You are jesting, sir! Surely you are!" And Fields sought to change the subject. "Can I get you a drink in the patio? How do you like California's gruesome sunshine?"

The gentleman shook his head. "Now about this picture? Or *these* pictures?" (Fields reported that his caller wagged a finger.) "Maybe you can dig up a *small* one, or maybe even *two* studies of a certain lady in Washington?"

The recollection of his ordeal of the morning brought sweat to our friend's broad face. He downed a triple martini, then went on to say that the government man's seeming knowledge of the miniatures had given him the jitters. "I envied all the dead," he declared, "including those who perished at Waterloo or the Galveston flood."

Fields had had no way of knowing, of course, that the government agent actually was an admirer of his talents and had no liking whatsoever for the lady of the miniatures. Then, quite suddenly—and Fields could not remember clearly just what caused him to change his mind—he sensed that the FBI man actually had come on a friendly mission.

"In a moment of boyish abandon," he told us, "or else I was in a trance, I brought out one of these little pictures from a desk drawer. I almost fell dead when the dear chappie burst out laughing. And do you know what?" Uncle Claude helped himself to another triple martini from a red rubber container fashioned to resemble a rum keg. "He asked if I would make him a present of the picture!"

"But you didn't do it?" said Decker.

"I still was leery of a trap"—the comedian blotted his brow with a bar towel—"for the government will strike down even a child and take away its marbles. Well, I had come up with some of the evidence so I decided to go the whole hog. I got the other two pictures and thrust them into his kindly hands."

"I hope he doesn't trace the miniatures to *me!*" Decker stroked his thin mustache.

"Buck up," said Fields. "He's not going to display 'em to

anybody till there's a change in the administration." He added grimly, "And if there's anything permanent in this life it's the administration."

We had more refreshments, and our host inquired, "How are you getting on with your friend Itchy-Britches or whatever his name is?"

"I've got him born," I said.

"That," replied Uncle Claude, "establishes a new world's record for midwives."

He rubbed his belly, beamed on us, then turned on an old-fashioned dictation machine that had on it a cylindrical wax record from which his secretary, Magda Michael, transcribed his letters. His name for this expert and amiable young woman was "Mickey Mouse."

"Mickey Mouse, cancel that letter I wrote to the Treasury Department," he said into the mouthpiece at one end of the flexible tube attached to the dictation machine. "The Treasury is full of no-good so-and-so's, but why knock the foot that rocks the hand that feeds the chickens that eat the daisies from off'n your grave?"

He clicked off the machine, went over to his wall slate, and wrote: "Squabs for dinner, with wild rice, and brandy gravy."

The next day I received a letter from W. C. Fields on the baby-blue stationery he always used, with a facsimile of his signature embossed in white at the upper left-hand corner of the paper. He wrote in part:

So you simply *will* fool around with this old moocher Catch-a-Crotchie. Why don't you get a job singing in

saloons instead? Singing in saloons is a more expensive
hobby than playing golf, polo, and, I was going to say,
horse-racing. You are a masochist—you derive pleasure
from making yourself suffer, and I am not going to be a
party to such damned nonsense. It grieves your friends
and myself to know that you continue on such a mad
career.

Do you remember when I was in Las Encinas and
was suffering from parethesia, and I remonstrated with
you for not gathering up the watches that it was my firm
belief I was pulling out from betwixt my fingers? You
told me the good doctors, Thompson and Smith, had informed you to tell me the truth; that if you did not I
would never get well. I am reciprocating this same kindness to you at this time. You have fooled around at
Hygeia's behest and advice without even obtaining a
modicum of success. You have suffered and your friends
have suffered with you. They and I all think you have a
very nice voice and we all love to hear you sing, but it is
not the kind of a voice that is going to make you the
kind of living you deserve. Get that old bounder out of
the city limits!

This is the end of the sermon. Amen!

F. F. F.

Father Faviana Fields.

As I sit at work in my writing room I see the various keepsakes that once belonged to my wonderful friends. I see Bill
Fields' black fedora, the four gay little feathers in the bow
of the hatband, which he wore at Barrymore's funeral, and
the crooked pool cue with which he had bashed Ed Wynn's
head when the two comedians performed together long ago
in the *Ziegfeld Follies*—when Wynn, from beneath the pool

table on-stage, had dared to steal laughs with his own pantomime.

A telegram arrives at my door. It is from Pat Young, wife
of that great little gentleman of the theater, Roland Young:
"Roland passed away quietly in his sleep last night."

There will be no more writing on my part today. Instead
I shall take cracked corn and breadcrumbs down to the blue
jay that is now my friend. The bird has learned to expect
this favor, and whenever I absent-mindedly fail to bring it
gifts scolds me outrageously.

For obvious reasons I have named this bird Sadakichi.

CHAPTER

FIVE

Winter? Spring? Who knows?
White buds from the plum trees wing,
And mingle with the snows.
No blue skies the flowers bring,
Yet their fragrance augurs spring.
                              —Sadakichi

My almost unreadable notes (I began life left-handed, but teachers who knew best imposed their orthodox runes upon me) make it difficult for me to decide whether it was in June or July of 1940 that Sadakichi, Decker, and I called at Barrymore's studio dressing room. Whatever the month or the day, we found Jack in a *Hamlet* costume, drinking Coca-Cola from one of a dozen bottles stacked in a tub of ice. He was waiting between scenes for a call to play a burlesque role in *The Great Profile*.

"I am contemplating a divorce," he informed me somewhat grimly, patting the dagger at his belt. "But let us not discuss hostilities at a social moment." He turned to greet his other guests. "Gentlemen, as my old minstrel friend George Primrose used to say, be seated."

"This costume"—Jack gestured with a bottle opener—"reminds me of the time brother Lionel played Macbeth. He went on a futuristic spree with the piece. When he asked me what was the matter with the production, why the critics had panned him so severely, I said, 'You've done everything but paint your scrotum green.' "

Sadakichi had been sniffing at one of the empty bottles. "There was something else in this. Eh?"

"The property man is a good friend of mine." Barrymore winked. "Spikes the medium with booze, recaps the pretty bottles, then brings 'em to me in this tub of ice. We are taking out a patent."

"Thought you were off the hard stuff?" said Decker.

"I shall quote Milton's phrase," Jack replied. " 'Hence with denial vain, and coy excuse.' " He then asked me, "Well, my sweet-scented bastard, how are you getting on with our noble Sadakichi's memoirs?"

"We have been exploring his Philadelphia days—from 1882 until 1885, to be exact."

"Excellent! Excellent!" The actor turned to Hartmann. "It seems we both arrived in Philadelphia the same year, only I came by way of the stork. Did you find it the city of brotherly, or perchance sisterly, love?"

"I knew absolutely nothing of sex or of business at that time," said Sadakichi. "Any objection?"

"None at all." Jack nodded in my direction. "Make copious notes. Our friend must have starved in several important ways."

"I did starve," said Sadakichi, "in all ways."

Upon his arrival in Philadelphia he had gone to the home of a granduncle in Buttonwood Street, where he was given lodgings in the attic. The granduncle found a job for him at three dollars a week as porter for a firm of lithographers, then charged him the three dollars for room and board.

Sadakichi went to night school in Philadelphia; frequented secondhand bookshops; and when his grandmother occasionally sent him a few dollars from Hamburg spent it all on books.

His granduncle died some nine months after Sadakichi's arrival. He moved away from Buttonwood Street, obtained a job with a tombstone designer, and after that became a retoucher of photographic negatives. In his off-hours he visited the Philadelphia Museum of Fine Arts, where he met Carl Weber, painter of sheep and apple blossoms.

"I also became the friend of a man who carved cigar-store Indians," said Sadakichi.

"As a model?" was Jack's mischievous inquiry.

To this Sadakichi retorted, "I knew your father. He was a much greater actor than you ever were. Hah!"

Barrymore laughed heartily and placed a spiked bottle in Sadakichi's hand. "If you were so hungry in Philadelphia, why didn't you call on my grandmother, Mrs. Drew? She fed whole regiments."

Sadakichi drank a toast to Mrs. Drew's memory. "She once gave me some cinnamon buns and milk and a pass to the Arch Street Theatre to see Edwin Booth." He could not resist another thrust at Jack. "Booth was a *real* actor."

"And so are you," said Jack. "But you were speaking of food, or the lack of it."

"The trouble is," Sadakichi said, "that people eat either too much or not enough. Half of humanity, or more, cannot afford varied and proper nourishment. The other half gorges itself into chronic dyspepsia. I am acquainted with both methods. I have starved in many cities; among them, Philadelphia, Boston, New York, Paris, San Francisco, and London. Of course, in London the cooking was so bad that it was much easier to do without food."

In Philadelphia he had hungered for days at a time. He recalled one ten-day fast during which he had had a loaf of stale bread, nothing else. "It was hard as a rock, that bread. I soaked it in water and munched small pieces until it was gone. On the third day the mind becomes deranged; one wishes to smash things or scream. Then follow periods of languor, a feeling of calmness and deep lethargy, with pains in the stomach at the accustomed meal hours. I had no fat to fall back upon. This ten-day fast, and others of lesser duration, contributed toward making me an invalid."

He interrupted the recital of his privations to say to me, "I want you to buy a coffin and send it to my house in Banning."

"Have you a tryst with Charon?" Decker asked.

"You cannot understand my desire for a coffin," said our hero. "Not with that sheepshead on your shoulders. Hah!"

"A coffin, eh?" Barrymore pretended great concern. "Until now I had assumed that the immortal Sadakichi would solo like Elijah in a flaming chariot." As an afterthought he added, "A vehicle donated by William Farnum or the fire-insured producers of *Ben Hur.*"

Sadakichi dismissed Jack's words with a contemptuous flick of the hand. "I shall use the coffin by day as a desk upon which to write poems and by night as a couch."

"He has a practical side after all," Decker observed.

Sadakichi returned to the subject of hunger. On one occasion during his Philadelphia days he received a remittance from his grandmother and bought books instead of food. He read all that night and late into the morning. He would have read on and on, but the smell of bread being baked by his landlady in the downstairs kitchen filtered through his meditations. "I found some relief," he said, "by reading a book on the famines of China."

The owner of a bookstore where Sadakichi frequently looked for bargains happened to find ten cents in stamps that Hartmann had mislaid on one of his visits. Since the young poet had not put in an appearance for the past ten days the bookseller sent an errand boy to Hartmann's place, with the stamps and a note to ask if he was ill.

Sadakichi invested the stamps in a mince pie, ate it, and became quite ill. "When I recovered," he said, "this bookstore man sent me to Camden to see his good friend Walt Whitman, greatest of modern prophets."

"Someone told me," Decker commented mischievously, "that Whitman gave you the brush-off."

This remark enraged Sadakichi. "Hearsay is the mother of discord," he rasped. "It appears that you would rather lose a friend than a jest. Hah!"

The next day, still piqued by Decker's reference to Whitman's anger, and without even saying "Hello" (meaning good-by, of course), Sadakichi vanished from his hotel. A clerk said his guest had cashed my weekly one-hundred-dollar check and left me a note scribbled in archaic but legible handwriting: "Get *two* coffins—one for yourself."

Several days later Decker, his wife Phyllis, and I motored to Banning to see the old fellow. This California town lies eighty-three miles southeast of Los Angeles, just this side of Palm Springs and the desert. There, on a blistering hot day, we found Sadakichi, wrapped in an overcoat, puttering and muttering outside his Indian reservation hut. We entered the shambles of his front yard by way of a makeshift gate, once the head of a wrought-iron bedstead. Sunbleached weeds and discarded tin cans surrounded the Hartmann hut; the barking of dogs sounded from a neighboring cluster of houses provided by the government for its wards.

Inside the house were two rooms instead of the one we had thought he occupied. He explained that a windstorm just recently had blown off the roof and turned it nicely edgewise inside the place. He had nailed this gift of the elements to the bare wall studs, then cut a doorway in it to make two rooms. There was a new roof, and Hartmann was preparing to give the exterior of the hut a coat of paint.

Our critic was in a vile mood because a mail-order company had sent him two one-gallon cans of paint of the wrong color. He had ordered blue, and both cans plainly bore the "Blue" label—but the pigment itself was an emerald green!

The old man permitted us to take him to a saloon beyond the "no alcohol" limits imposed by government regulations. At the saloon he forgot about the green paint and his other problems, drank, danced, and even made peace when a derrick worker from the oil fields threatened to punch Decker in the nose.

That night, at the Banning hotel, Sadakichi again spoke of his Whitman days. He assessed me fifty dollars for a typed copy of his thirteen-thousand-word pamphlet *Conversations with Walt Whitman* (published in 1895).

This pamphlet was an expanded version of an article written by Sadakichi in 1887 for the *New York Herald*. The newspaper account had caused the Good Gray Poet much embarrassment, it is said. Hartmann had quoted Whitman in regard to several contemporary men of letters, and these quotations had irked the poet. Among them were the following: "Emerson's deficiency is that he doubts everything." And of Oliver Wendell Holmes: "He serves his humor in a dainty fashion. Witty, smart; not first rank and not second rank." And of Mark Twain: "It seems to me as if he produces nothing new. An imitator. Was Washington Irving anything but a clever English essayist?" And, worst of all to Whitman's way of thinking, Hartmann's version of what the poet said of Stedman: "He is after all nothing but a sophisticated dancing master. If Hercules or Apollo himself would make their appearance, Stedman would look at them only from the standpoint of a dancing master."

In a yellowed newspaper clipping of uncertain origin but upon which I saw penciled-in September 14, 1888—a relic Sadakichi refused to part with, even for ten dollars, but permitted me to copy for a fee to that amount—Whitman was quoted as having said, "I have more hopes of Hartmann, more faith in him than in any of the boys. They all seem to

regard him as a humbug—or if not that, a sensationalist any-
how, or an adventurer. I can't see it that way. I expect good
things from him—extra good things; not great, but good.
The Boston fellows seem to be particularly strong against
him: some of them seem to think that if he is not a bad egg,
he is at least the raw stuff of a bad egg. That sounds very
familiar: lots of the most amiable people have from time to
time anonymously written me the same facts about myself."

Then, as if to reverse his favorable opinion of Sadakichi
(perhaps Whitman meantime had read the *Herald* article),
the old poet was quoted in a subsequent newspaper clipping (this one cost me a fiver) as having said, "But there
was Hartmann—he too did some business of the reporting
sort. He gave some of his notes to Kennedy [Dr. William
Sloan Kennedy], who sent them to me. They were absurdly
warped: everything that should have been straight was
crooked. He put Carlylean fire in my mouth—made me sat-
urnine: said things for me I didn't say for myself."

In 1940 I received a letter from John G. Moore, a Whitman admirer. He possessed numerous letters and papers
from the estate of one of Whitman's friends, a Dr. Wiksell.
I was unable at the time thoroughly to pursue this lead; and
now, after a lapse of years, I find it inexpedient to try to
locate Mr. Moore or his papers. Probably—as so often happens—these and other pertinent matters will be freely supplied after this book appears between hard covers. Meantime I can only offer circumstantial evidence, with here and
there some documentation.

Dr. Wiksell wrote Mr. Moore that Whitman cursed Sadakichi as "that damned Japanese." I have read somewhere

that Whitman never used strong language, except in his published descriptions of the human anatomy, but I leave this matter to the scholars to determine.

"After Walt read the Hartmann fantasy," Dr. Wiksell reported, "the old man cursed again, then calmed down; for he was always unable to prevent his curses ever being without a corresponding blessing. After a while Walt said, 'Bless his heart. He meant well.'"

The first interview appeared in the *New York Herald* during Whitman's lifetime. Then, in 1895, Hartmann issued the pamphlet that drew the fire of many Whitmanites, including T. B. Harnel of Camden, who wrote to Sadakichi in part: "It is not fair to reprint this after Whitman's death. The article caused considerable trouble when it was first published. Walt repudiated the whole article and told me that you had manufactured it. You made him call Stedman a 'sophisticated dancing master,' and this caused no end of mischief. Walt had the greatest possible regard for Stedman, and there was a strong attachment between these two men. Walt assured Stedman that you had coined the expression out of your own unaided imagination."

Of this Hartmann said to me, "Hah! Whitman didn't give a damn what anyone said about him either in the way of praise or attack."

Whitman in his last years had yet another complaint against Sadakichi: the impulsive young man had bobbed up in New England to establish a Walt Whitman Society to solicit funds for the aged poet. Hartmann, of course, had appointed himself treasurer.

"Whittier gave me five dollars for the Whitman Society,"

Sadakichi told me at Banning, "but was worried lest such patronage, if generally known, might cause the public to think that he approved of Whitman's realistic descriptions of the human body. Whittier had on a long linen duster the day I called on him. He gave me five silver dollars but warned, 'I want it clearly understood that my name is not to be mentioned in connection with Walt's.' " Sadakichi added sardonically, "His name never *will* be mentioned with Whitman's."

There is contemporary evidence that Whitman objected to the formation of a group that had as its intention, however disguised or sugar-coated, to make of him a recipient of charity. *The Critic* (September issue, 1888) said that "Hartmann attempted to launch a Walt Whitman Society on an unprepared world." Whitman was quoted in rebuttal: "A world unprepared! Yes indeed! But I was the fellow who put his foot down on that little plan—who forbade the launching of the enterprise. . . . But Hartmann is more than the organizer of the Whitman club. . . . His views on things Occidental, as they say, are rare, novel—should be heard. . . . He has written astonishingly good studies . . . surprisingly searching—some of them."

Whatever doubts may obtain as to Sadakichi's quotations of Walt Whitman, he managed to supply a word-picture of the old genius and his Camden residence that surpasses, to my way of thinking, most descriptions offered by chroniclers of the poet's evening.

It was in November of 1884 that Hartmann paid the first of his many visits to Whitman. The caller was then in his nineteenth year, and so great was his excitement that he took the wrong ferryboat across the Delaware River from Philadelphia to Camden and landed some distance upstream from Whitman's two-story frame house on Mickle Street.

It was a disagreeable day, Hartmann recalled, with the snow thawing under a strong wind. In reply to his knock the front door opened, and Sadakichi saw standing before him an old man with a long gray beard spread over his naked breast.

"I would like to see Walt Whitman."

"That's my name. And you are a Japanese boy, are you not?"

"My father is German, but my mother was a Japanese."

Sadakichi reported the scene in part as follows: "He led me into the small and humble two-windowed little parlor, with its chilly atmosphere, as no fire was lit, and everything in great disorder. The first color impression of the interior was a frugal gray.

"He sat down at the right-hand window, where he was generally to be seen by outsiders, with his face turned toward the street. Inside the parlor a visitor would sit on the opposite side of the room. Between host and guest stood a table covered with books, magazines, circulars, manuscripts, piled in topsy-turvy fashion; and here and there odd pieces of furniture, a trunk, a large heap of his own publications, loomed up like rocks.

"On the mantelpiece stood an old clock surrounded by photographs of celebrities and friends. At the time of my first visit apples and onions were scattered about on the mantel. At one side of it hung a portrait of his father, and on the other side that of his mother: two strong, highly interesting physiognomies.

"'I never forget that my ancestors were Dutch,'" Sadakichi quoted Whitman as having said to him.

Hartmann liked Whitman's face for its healthy manliness and said that the poet's complexion was as rosy as a baby's. "Above all else," Sadakichi continued, "I was attracted by the free flow of his gray hair and beard and the distance between his heavy eyebrows and his bluish-gray eyes, calm and cold in their expression, denoting frankness, boldness, haughtiness. His forehead was broad and massive, not furrowed by Kantian meditation but rather vaulted by spontaneous prophecies. His broad nose with its dilated nostrils showed with what joy of living he had inhaled life."

Whitman at this time had recovered to a degree from the paralytic stroke suffered in 1873 and now got about with the aid of a yellow stick. Until his last years he would go to Philadelphia on occasion to see a play at Mrs. Drew's Arch Street Theatre; or, as Hartmann wrote in an article for the *Southwest Review* (1927), to walk slowly along the streets, his left foot dragging, and reply to all greetings in a cordial manner. Whitman was not a talkative person, however, Hartmann reported, and had a habit of replying with an "Oy! Oy!" to most questions.

Before the *Herald* article Sadakichi served occasionally as a letter-writer for Whitman. He would translate and then reply to greetings sent the poet in the German language. The Whitman experience seems to have given Sadakichi a taste for getting into the good graces (and then, of course, out of them) of many men of public note. He had access, because of the letters, to a "Who's Who" of the poet's famous correspondents abroad.

Blessed with a roster of such names as Maurice Maeterlinck, Mallarmé, Heyse, Pierre Loti, Zola, and a number of others, and with a most retentive memory for confidence-inspiring details drawn from the letters, young Hartmann felt he could hit the jackpot, so to speak, of immediate friendly acceptance in European salons. He begged, borrowed, connived, sold his books, and even denied himself food to accumulate funds for the enterprise.

Fortunately for him there was an amazing rate-war going on among the steamship companies. For the ridiculously cheap price of seven dollars he not only obtained passage, third class on the Red Star Line, from New York to Antwerp, Belgium, but, oddly enough, his railroad fare from Philadelphia to New York as well. After a night at the Astor House in downtown New York he was advised by a genial stranger to go to a money exchange on the Bowery, where he could turn his greenbacks into French money at a great advantage to him.

With the zeal of a big-game hunter, he left for Europe in 1885, to begin his first safari in search of artistic lions.

After a fifteen-day voyage through stormy February seas, during which he slept with his clothes on and his hands in his pockets to keep his many coins from rolling to the steerage deck, he arrived in Antwerp.

At the Hotel Antoine, an expensive place for those days, he engaged a room, ordered soap and a bath, dressed in a clean spare suit, and proceeded to the dining room to have the best of wine and food. He next went to the Opera House, where *The Huguenots* was billed. When he put down two of his five-franc pieces for a box seat the ticket-seller sent for the police. These, and all other pieces of money he had obtained at the Bowery exchange, were counterfeit.

Sadakichi managed to explain his way out of jail, pawned his valise, and borrowed enough money from an American traveler to go third class to Hamburg. There his grandmother fed him, outfitted him with new clothes and luggage, and paid his railway fare to Paris.

He may have traveled third class on the steamship and the railway, but he traveled first class in the salons of members of the Academy—until ejected.

"They couldn't stand his pipe," Barrymore said. "It was Vesuvius, with halitosis."

A thousand years may pass
Till this fir bends to decay.
Fair morning-glory,
Content with a single day,
Do you mourn your shorter stay?
                              —Sadakichi

A week after the journey to Banning I was called from my garden to answer the telephone. A faint-voiced Sadakichi was at the other end of the line. "I'm dying of starvation."

"Where are you?"

"At Decker's."

John and Phyllis Decker had gone to Camp Baldy for the July Fourth holiday.

"I'll be right down," I said. "I have some bacon, eggs, milk. How about peanut butter?"

"Too common." And he hung up with a "Hah!"

I found the old fellow hunched over on the couch, with one of Decker's blankets draped over him. He had taken out his false teeth, and his jaws were flexing like a bellows.

I scorched the bacon and eggs in the frying pan.

"With my last breath"—Sadakichi paused to put in his

store teeth—"I will testify that your cooking is as bad as your writing."

I was about to inquire how he had managed to get into the house, but the answer to my unasked question was the ripped screen of the kitchen window. "Sadakichi, I must have given you at least sixty dollars in Banning. How could you have gone hungry?"

He gestured with a fork but otherwise ignored my question. "When in Paris in eighteen eighty-five," he said, "while writing my erotic poem 'Naked Ghosts,' I met Paul Verlaine for the first time at the Café François Premier. The poet was waiting to be treated to pure green absinthe, a drink he liked to take one after the other. One night when leaving Mallarmé's I met him again, and we wandered all about the strange places of Paris. The next morning, in some little restaurant on the outskirts of the city, we drank wonderful white wine as the laborers were going to work. One of the incidents that make life worth living at all."

When he had finished eating he told me that he had collapsed in his Banning hut after our call, had hemorrhaged profusely, lost consciousness, and lain for three days and nights on the floor, without food or water. He was unsure of just how he had managed to get out of his house and come to Bundy Drive.

Dr. Hirshfeld arrived at Decker's. He placed a stethoscope to Sadakichi's chest. He found the heart remarkably sound but the bronchial inflammation severe. The doctor recommended hospitalization, but the stubborn old fellow would have none of that. "Just invent something for my asthma."

Dr. Hirshfeld prescribed a liquid that contained a morphine derivative. Instead of taking it a teaspoonful at a time, as directed, Hartmann emptied the four-ounce bottle by nightfall. He then asked me to have the prescription refilled. I consulted Dr. Hirshfeld by telephone. "Nothing doing," he said. "I'm not a dope peddler."

The Deckers returned home from Mount Baldy the afternoon of the Fourth. John put on some old clothes, fed his chickens, and began to gather plums from a backyard tree. Sadakichi reclined nearby on a beach chair. With a rusted flyswatter in his hand he was keeping time to "The Dance of the Hours," coming over Decker's portable radio. When the music stopped Sadakichi got up to leave the yard.

We thought he had gone to the bathroom. He was away for so long that we searched the premises—and found him among an array of antique picture frames stored in the garage. Seated behind a gilt frame, he looked like one of those living pictures shown at the annual Laguna Festival.

"It's the first authentic portrait," he said, "of the hundreds that have been made of me."

Toward evening Thomas Mitchell dropped in with a bottle for Sadakichi. The old man astonished us by declining to drink, demanding orange ice instead. Phyllis said that the soda fountains were closed for the day.

Jack Barrymore, accompanied by a male nurse (a man who sometimes acted as his chauffeur, big Karl Stuevers), arrived as Sadakichi was denouncing me for having failed to buy him a coffin. He wanted one with a slipcover made of summery material and with a gay design on it.

"I tried to get that coffin for you," I said. "In fact I consulted Harry Brand, our obliging publicity-director friend at Fox. Harry said it's against the law for wholesalers to sell a coffin to anyone but morticians. The undertakers also cannot retail a box—unless, of course, there is a properly signed death certificate."

"Then have the doctor write the certificate," Sadakichi demanded. "I'm as good as dead."

Dr. Hirshfeld telephoned to report that Sadakichi's bleeding spells might be controlled by a newly found vitamin, not yet on the market. "It can be supplied, to some extent, by eating lemon peel. Better still, stew the lemon peel and have him drink the residual liquor."

The sun began to set, and Decker, who couldn't stand the sight of it, went indoors to see how his roast beef was faring. He had something to drink with various callers—Roland Young and Anthony Quinn—and then decided to make some dumplings. Quinn went home to study a script, but Young stayed on at Decker's insistence.

"You are the glass of courtesy," Decker said to Roland. "And you should always have something in such a fine glass."

The dinner late that night was not exactly a success. Decker's dumplings fell, not once, but twice, during their preparation. At this mishap our host went into a rage. He threatened to destroy all his paintings in a fit of artistic hara-kiri, spoke disparagingly of his late mother, and predicted the end of the world come the next March.

During this storm Sadakichi remained very calm. "I am a man of violent actions but of spirit serene. I once pulled down a chandelier on the head of a heckler in a Greenwich Village café, then threw his brother-in-law down the stairs.

But I stayed perfectly serene." He gummed a lemon peel, then announced that his weight had fallen off to a hundred and thirty-two pounds.

"With or without your truss?" asked Barrymore.

"Hello!" He leered at Jack. His "hello" meant, as we have remarked some pages ago, a not so good "good-by." He turned to Mitchell. "You are the one bright mind in the place. Decker would like me to praise his skill as a painter, but he'll have to wait a long time for that. Let us discuss the great moments of stage literature."

He spoke of Ibsen's ability to dramatize nature as of a shaft of light reaching through a window. Then he described the stage in Budapest, its many mechanical contrivances, and the stages of the Munich royal theaters, the Hof and the Residenz.

In April of 1885, and for some months thereafter, he had served as an apprentice of stagecraft at the Hof Theatre. Among his duties was the hoisting of the evening star in *Tannhäuser*. Richard Wagner formerly had presided at the Hof Theatre under the aegis of the eccentric Ludwig, the Swan King; but when Hartmann arrived in Munich the composer had been dead two years.

Ludwig, now fat and completely mad, would appear at dress rehearsals given at his command and on short notice; then, hidden from view, the royal maniac would shout criticisms and insults at the actors. "A year, or perhaps a little less, before the king drowned himself in Starnberger Lake," Sadakichi said, "he ordered what was to be his last dress rehearsal of *Parsifal*. He sat alone in the royal box, with red drapes and screens hung or placed all about him. There were apertures through which he would peer down on the singers.

"We apprentices, as well as the shifters of scenes, were required to wear felt coverings over our boots at this rehearsal. The theater proper was kept in darkness; and the king didn't arrive by carriage from Neuschwanstein until after midnight. I crept near to the royal box, for, surprisingly enough, the king had no bodyguards. I always have had very good eyes in the dark. I studied him for a long time. He belched a great deal."

Sadakichi now addressed Barrymore. "I had seen many portraits that represented Ludwig as a young man. They were so unlike the fat, crazed monarch I spied upon. Obviously he had been quite handsome; and I am still amazed as I think back to the early portraits, which made him look almost exactly as you do in the *Hamlet* photographs, features and all."

This was the only time I saw Barrymore show his displeasure at anything Sadakichi said or did. The actor straightened in his chair. A sudden paleness of his cheeks gave a contrasting emphasis to the fierce brightness of his eyes. He spoke slowly, as though to underplay a scene of considerable moment. "Just what are you meaning to imply, sir, by your 'features and *all*' remark?"

The overshadowing dread that plagued this courageous man, as some of us knew, was his fear of becoming insane. In his youth he had seen his own father go into a mental eclipse. That tragedy had been unforgettable, he once told me; and somehow he expected a like fate.

Sadakichi, for once, was unable to reply to the challenge. Decker managed to relieve the tension by referring to an incident of recent occurrence, a situation involving Barrymore and an actress of his acquaintance.

"I hear that you were thrown out of Miss So-and-So's house," he said to Jack and named the woman.

Barrymore's good temper returned as he described the actress and her dream of one day appearing with him in *Macbeth* at the Hollywood Bowl.

"I called on her," Jack continued, "to find her dear little mother there—as a duenna, perhaps. The old lady was playing a game of Patience with the smallest cards I have ever seen. She merely nodded to me when I was introduced; she didn't speak a word the whole evening. She seemed not even to be listening as I outlined my theories about the play; for instance, I would not show the three witches but instead, as the curtain rises slowly, disclose a huge papier-mâché hand suspended over a kettle, the long forefinger stirring the brew, and only the voices of the unseen witches coming over.

"Well," Jack said wryly, "I happened to remark that I would play Macbeth in kilts, without a stitch of underwear; a very masculine as well as an ambitious Scot, ready to deal with female friend or male foe. My description seemed to bring the little old lady to life, and then to stun her. She leaned over the card table and forgot to play her black knave.

"To reassure the dazed dowager as to my artistic probity, I went over to her and inadvertently tapped her too hard on the back. She sprawled across the table, spilling the cards in all directions. Her lovely daughter promptly canceled all plans for *Macbeth* with a gesture of dismissal and the words, 'Please leave my house at once! You have insulted my mother!' "

During "the Monster's" recital Decker had been rummaging among his books. He seemed delighted to have come upon a high-school edition of *Macbeth*. "Gentlemen," he said, "we shall have a performance here and now of the Bard's great tragedy. But in modern dress, of course."

Mitchell excused himself to his hostess—perhaps because Sadakichi had spoken disparagingly of one of the pictures in his valuable collection, a Whistler "Nocturne," as I recall.

"This Hartmann can be a most disagreeable fellow," Mitchell said in a loud aside to Phyllis at the front door. "A rot-gut art critic at best."

"Good night then," Decker called out to him. "Go on home, you fat Borgian!"

Mitchell later told me that during his long walk home he kept thinking, over and over, "I must reduce! I must reduce!"

It should be explained, perhaps, that epithets fell on all sides, and at any time, at the Bundy Drive studio; anyone who could not protect himself in the clinches, as it were, was out of luck. Mitchell and Decker always remained the best of friends. The actor frequently rescued the artist from his creditors, bought pictures from him during hard times, commissioned him, at a good price, to decorate tiles for the fireplaces of his Oregon ranch, and otherwise stood by him and believed in his abilities.

After Mitchell deserted the cast it was decided that Sada-

kichi play the name role. Barrymore said he would be happy
to support Hartmann as Macduff. "By the word support"—
he arched a brow—"I mean only in tonight's theatricals, and
not in private life." Then he asked, "May I also play the
part of Fleance? He was a bearer of bad news."

"We shall see," said Decker. "We want only first-rate
talent." He then instructed Roland Young, "You will have
to double, or even triple, as Banquo, Duncan, and the
Witches."

"Who is to play Lady Macbeth?" asked Roland.

"The part should go to W. C. Fields," Barrymore said,
"now that Carrie Nation is dead."

"W. C. is asleep by this time," said Decker. "So I'll play
Lady Macbeth myself. Fowler, you will read all the bit
parts—lords, gentlemen, officers, murderers, and apparitions."

"I'll do nothing of the sort," I said.

"And why not?"

"Because I'm the audience."

"Then," said Decker, "we'll dispense with the bit parts entirely."

The one high-school book was not enough for the players.
We made telephone calls around and about; were cursed by
some of our friends for disturbing their rest and threatened
by others with dogs and guns if we so much as dared to
move our theatrical project to certain mansions of the
mighty. Barrymore's "keeper" went on a midnight mission to
the homes of a few amiable actor-neighbors, to solicit copies
of *Macbeth.*

While Karl was away Decker entertained us with a series
of impersonations. He did his own version of Abraham Lin-

coln freeing the slaves; he dressed for the part in Barrymore's old opera hat and a shawl once worn by Barrymore in the silent picture *Beau Brummel,* and glued a patch of fur to his chin. After that he did a characterization of Uriah Heep and an impersonation of Sadakichi, with flour applied to his face and crayon lines to give him a cadaverous appearance.

Decker, as a matter of fact, had the natural gifts of a good actor. His voice was deep and resonant, his enunciation splendid—a bit on the Barrymore side, for Jack was his idol.

Had he not undergone an unfortunate experience in his New York days, Decker might have won a place in the show world. In 1922 he was hired by stage-director Bert Angeles to perform in *The Fantastic Fricassee* at the Greenwich Village Theatre. That was Decker's first appearance as an actor, and also his last. At his then age of twenty-six years, Decker had not yet become a drinking man. At curtain time a great fright came over him. A member of the cast gave him two drinks of bootleg whisky. He went on-stage, but as he tried to deliver his first line fell across the footlights and into the orchestra pit. The curtain was rung down.

Soon after this damp episode he obtained a job as a theatrical cartoonist on the *New York Evening World,* and in the course of that work became acquainted with Sadakichi and Barrymore.

Karl returned at last with two copies of *Macbeth,* one of them Volume III of my own set of Shakespeare, printed in 1803 from the text of "Mr. Steevens's Last Edition."

"For you." I offered the book to Sadakichi.

He handed it back to me. "Too heavy. Would interfere with my gestures."

"What in hell do you expect?" asked Decker. "A first folio?"

Barrymore was delighted to accept the authoritative text of Mr. Steevens. "Nothing is too heavy for me—except matrimony."

"Please, gentlemen!" said Decker, the opera hat on his head, his face still covered with flour, and the shawl draped about his shoulders.

"Perhaps," Barrymore suggested to Decker, "you should play Lady Macbeth without the opera hat. Unless, of course, you see her as the mannish type. And, come to think of it, she was."

The artist put aside the hat, gave Sadakichi the high-school text, and offered to share the other with Roland Young—a volume that belonged, if I am not mistaken, to Cesar Romero, who lived up the way from Decker's studio.

"Obviously," said the artist, "we shall have to read our parts. Barrymore isn't the only one among us with the memory of a sieve."

"I can remember *Macbeth* distinctly," Jack declared. "Almost word for word."

"Then," said I, "why do you need the idiot boards on the set?"

"My learned friend," Jack said to me, "I remember Shakespeare's words because he was a great writer. I can't remember Hollywood lines; just as I may well recall a wonderful meal at Delmonico's many years ago, but not the contents of the garbage pail last Tuesday at Joe's Fountain Grill."

"We are getting nowhere," Decker said.

"Nowhere," agreed Sadakichi, "and that is the ideal place to be." He made some quick gestures, the fingers of one hand fluttering over the back of the other hand.

"Now what, for the love of Moses, are *you* doing?" Decker asked Hartmann. "Got the itch?"

Sadakichi, still moving his fingers, explained, "Even the most stupid observer should know that my right hand is Hamlet. My left is Ophelia. Thank you very much."

"But dammit," Decker shouted, "what is Hamlet doing in *Macbeth*?"

"What are *you* doing in it?" asked Hartmann, and he did a little dance.

"Now," said Decker, "let us turn to page nineteen."

He seemingly lost sight of the fact that page nineteen of his book was not the same, in terms of dialogue and action, as that page in Jack's book or in Sadakichi's high-school version.

A lively dispute came of this. Decker had chosen to begin at Lady Macbeth's entrance in Scene VI, before the castle, after Duncan (Roland Young) says, "See! See! Our honour'd hostess!" etc.

Page nineteen of Barrymore's book began halfway through the soliloquy in Scene VII, a room in the castle, with Macbeth declaiming, "If it were done when 'tis done, then 'twere well it were done quickly," etc.

Sadakichi's book, page nineteen, had on it Macbeth saying to Duncan, "The service and the loyalty I owe, in doing it pays itself."

As individualists of strong will, each of the actors—except Roland Young, who was a gentleman at all times—began to read aloud from his respective page nineteen. The Tower of Babel must have been exactly like this.

Decker quite abruptly put down his book and asked Sadakichi to acknowledge his gifts as a painter. The old fellow merely spread his hands in a gesture of dismissal.

Many critics, among them Arthur Millier and Dr. W. R. Valentiner, had praised Decker's work, but he seemed obsessed by the desire to win Hartmann's approval. "Why don't you ever come through for me?" Decker shouted at Sadakichi. "You know damned well that my work is beautiful!"

"When you cease being a caricaturist," said the old man, "then knock at my door. I may let you in. We'll see."

This rejoinder precipitated so much loud bickering that neighbors complained of the disturbance. Decker's dogs began to bark. Barrymore sang "Blow the Man Down." A desk-sergeant of the West Los Angeles police telephoned us "to pipe down, or else."

Young and I departed in his car at about four o'clock in the morning. Roland dropped me off at my house, up the hill on Barrington, and said in parting, "Decker, and *not* Macbeth, does murder sleep."

Though Life has grown cold,
The woods are bright with flowers.
Why not, as of old,
Go to the wildwood bowers
And dream of bygone hours?
                        —Sadakichi

On a hot noonday in July 1940 John Decker telephoned from Hartmann's hotel to say, "Sadakichi is on the
floor with a hemorrhage."

"Call Dr. Hirshfeld, and wait there for me," I said.

Dr. Samuel Hirshfeld was a many-sided practitioner,
mindful at all times of the weaknesses that too often beset
talented men. We called him Sam, and told him our secrets.
Because of our blindness to signs of his tiring heart—for no
one, it seems, thinks his doctor has the right to become ill—
we quickened Sam's end with our round-the-clock demands.

Ben Hecht said at his funeral, "I never knew a man whose
soul was so kind and whose mind so tender. I never knew
a man who shed so bright a smile upon the world, all of it—
the rich world and the poor world; the too clever and the
too stupid world. He was not a man to discriminate. He was
a man so rich that he gave to all whether they deserved it or

not. And there lay his one flaw: he gave too much away. He finally gave it all away."

Over the years I had sent more than a hundred non-paying patients to this doctor, or called him to their beds. He even treated the pets of his friends, for he had a wonderful way with animals. However, he always enjoined us to keep it quiet that he was competing with the veterinarians.

When my duck Montmorency was mauled by dogs one day, its wing broken, and its breast feathers almost gone, Sam adjusted the broken wing. Montmorency floated in the bathtub for the diagnosis as well as the treatment and sounded a grateful "Quack! Quack!"

"Someone is paging you, Sam," I said mischievously.

"Dammit!" he exclaimed. "If you breathe a word about this I'll never treat another of your seedy friends."

At the hotel, this hot July day, I found Sadakichi sitting up in bed. He had on his overcoat, as usual, and was nibbling at a lemon peel, then spitting the pulp into a nearby wastebasket.

"Sadakichi," I said, "won't you let me take you to the hospital?"

Ignoring my suggestion, he began to speak of his Munich days. "I wanted to be an actor—a singer too. But I couldn't sing, so I learned to dance. In later lustrums I was able to express myself in improvisatory fashion to any music I clearly heard, never getting out of time."

When the doctor arrived Sadakichi merely flicked his hand in greeting and went right on with his memories. "I liked to watch the ballet girls when they rehearsed or did their exercises at the bar, the half-split and the other de-

lightful contortions; for the privacy of their undress, I had
to make use of holes in the dressing-room door. It was a true
Degas atmosphere."

"Let's get rid of this overcoat," the doctor said, "so that I
may examine your chest."

Sadakichi gestured that he would not permit Dr. Hirshfeld to remove the coat and continued with his spoken
thoughts of the past. "No amatory adventures troubled me,
although I was surrounded every evening by girls in tights.
I hardly ever spoke to them. Ah! Opportunities do not come
at the right moment. Now I wouldn't in the least mind being
amidst a bevy of buxom, sturdy-legged German *Fräuleins*.
The love duet in *Tristan und Isolde* was still a strange language to me, and I preferred to gaze at young coryphees
struggling with tights and bodices. It was worship from
afar."

Dr. Hirshfeld took me aside. "The one thing that seems
to keep this old fellow alive, other than his strong heart, is
the importance that you waggish gentlemen are giving
him."

"Giving him!" I exclaimed. "He's *demanding* it."

"Well, whatever the situation, he has thrived on trouble
all his life—even invited it—and the more you challenge him,
the better he likes it."

"Say, do you think he's nuts?"

"Not in the clinical sense. But, as Ben Hecht has said, most
artists are maniacs."

We returned to Sadakichi's bedside to find him communi-
cating with Decker by means of his own kind of sign language.

"Kichi," the artist was saying, "would you pose for a last picture, the Dying Half-Teuton?"

The great exhibitionist responded at once to this invitation. He got out of bed, much against Sam's advice, even took off his overcoat, and in his green undershirt and dark gray drawers took a jack-knife position in an orange-upholstered chair. Decker posed him against a background grouping of an ice bowl, a bottle of medicine, two books, and a lemon on a wall shelf.

Once again I recommended that either he go to a hospital, or allow me to provide a male nurse at his Banning home. He denounced me as a corn-tassel Samaritan. "Would you rob me of this, my last chance to dramatize myself? Would you hide me in a hospital? Or commit me to the desert with an audience of coyotes, lizards, rattlesnakes, and pack rats? No! I shall die in public, as befits a great man and an enemy of the public."

The doctor decided to administer a hypodermic, and in half an hour or so Sadakichi fell asleep, mumbling now and then before the drug gave him surcease from pain.

The next day he seemed much improved. He put on a new outfit, a green ensemble Decker and I had bought for him, and announced that he would call upon the widow of an artist whose work he once had thought quite promising. The now middle-aged woman lived in straitened circumstances; her late husband's canvases hung on the walls of the otherwise bleakly furnished rooms. She had made lampshades out of cones of old newspapers.

We left Sadakichi at her house. That night she visited him at his hotel for several hours, dined and wined there, then left at midnight. On the way to the bus she stepped in the way of an automobile and was instantly killed.

Upon hearing of this next morning I dropped in at Sada-kichi's with the intention of consoling him. I was amazed to find him in one of his "serene" moods, apparently untroubled, and dictating his theories of rhythms in color to the secretary.

"Aren't you moved at all by this tragedy?" I inquired. "I thought it would upset even you."

"Quite the opposite," he said. "I envy her. First of all, she had the privilege of spending her last hours with Sadakichi Hartmann, and of hearing conversation denied to all but a fortunate few; and then going out of life suddenly, before the troubles and the dull words of an environment of fools could break her last enchantment."

With an impatient wave of the hand he closed that part of the discussion and for no reason that I could make out began to criticize me for having written *Illusion in Java*. "What makes you poor nomads think you can ride into any of these exotic countries and capture the real meaning of them or their people when all you do is drink coconut milk, look at a few dances you can by no means understand, hear a little native music, go home and write silly metaphors, and think you are the historians of culture? Why in hell do you dabble in a literature that has nothing for you, and you have nothing for it, when you are a simple peasant of the Western world?"

"What would you suggest I do about it?"

"Please write of the Western world." He paused to leer at me. "Or, better still, stop writing entirely."

He gazed out of a window that gave upon a view of the Hollywood jail. "I once spent two days in that ignoble pile. And it looks as bad inside as it does from here."

The next day Hartmann had a relapse. I located Sam by telephone at the hospital, where he had performed three operations in succession, with no rest between times except to scrub. He told me that his hamstrings were cramped from bending over the surgical table for seven hours. Notwithstanding his fatigue, Sam lugged his clinical case—a large one, it was—to Sadakichi's hotel, only to find that Hartmann had gone on a joy ride with a sculptor friend while I was away from the hotel for half an hour on an errand of my own.

Sam was understandably annoyed. "I told him not to risk another bleeding attack by jolting about in motorcars."

When Sadakichi returned to the hotel to learn that Sam had left, and had been annoyed by the wasted call, he snarled, "Who is *he* to be annoyed? I can't sit here waiting all day for these doctors, and besides they know nothing. What I want is some morphine. If they can't give me that, tell them to keep away from here."

His auto ride had been taken not only for pleasure but to visit a cemetery, from which one might see a large "H" made of concrete near the crest of a hill. (No one seems to know what the "H" stands for, except that Southern Californians like to autograph their highlands.) "They were expecting me," he said, "and dedicated the mountain to Hartmann."

The doctor stopped in to see Sadakichi once again on his way home. He administered a strong sedative but refused to accede to the patient's request for a popcorn bag of morphine tablets. Before the drug could take effect Hartmann

voiced his disappointment at this by dictating a long protest
to the secretary. "When a man is in his dying seventies," his
philippic charged, "and spilling blood from every pore; struggling like a hooked shark and utterly tired of the scheme
of things; what, I ask you, in the name of all the devils in
hell, difference does it make if he sniffs cocaine, chews
opium, smokes hashish, or has enough morphine needles to
make him look like a porcupine? What difference does it
make? Who cares whether you become an addict or not?
Does my lack of suffering, by means of a well-placed needle,
cause the government or the state any pain? Does it cause
the preachers in their pulpits to swoon with severe fistulas?
Does it do any harm to the Daughters of the American Revo-
lution? What can you expect from a nation that pays more
attention to robbing a dying man of bodily ease than it does
to making preparations against the invasion of an enemy?
These may be my dying words, as indeed I hope they are;
and I can assign to all the fires of hell the polliwog brains
that are at the head of the so-called Health Service! Damn
them all!"

In a characteristic *non sequitur* of thought and expression
he said sleepily, "If you think vaudeville is dead, look at
modern art."

The old man stayed on at the hotel for a few weeks, dictating notes on his life and editing the proofs of a pamphlet
called *Strands and Ravelings of the Art Fabric.* I had volunteered to seek a publisher for this monograph, but Hartmann said no, he would have it printed himself and sell it
through the mails. His project cost me five hundred dollars

but was worth the price, if only for his descriptions of the clash between the artistic and the materialistic ways of life, such as: "Mule and thoroughbred do not pull well together."

He attacked what he called the "Farley Dynasty," the murals painted under government subsidy by otherwise unemployed artists on the walls of post offices and public buildings. "Talent," Hartmann said of the muralists, "seems to be as scarce among them as pork in a can of beans. But for that matter I have not met anyone of importance these last twenty years, simply because there aren't any men of importance."

Many years before, Hartmann, as an upstart beginner at art criticism, had named a dozen artists whose work most likely would be acclaimed by the next generation: Albert Ryder, Abbott Thayer, Winslow Homer, Thomas Eakins, John La Farge, George Inness, Homer Martin, D. W. Tryon, Augustus Saint-Gaudens, and "if the Muses permit, Childe Hassam when he does not paint nudes" and Horatio Walker "when he paints pigs."

"Well," Sadakichi said, "the young critic made few errors, omissions, or overestimates. The choice was correct and my words came true."

Although he wrote in behalf of art and artists for almost fifty years (including a two-volume work, *A History of American Art*), Hartmann was mindful that these men sometimes regarded themselves and their talents from overprecious points of view.

"The great artists," he said, "are always the great givers; and we can give them little in return, as we do not even know who they are until they are dead. They know in a way; but no genius can be absolutely sure that he is one (except in my case) or that posterity will think him so. Most artists have the failing of considering themselves greater than they are. Why talk of geniuses? They do not sit at your elbow; they are scarce; there are only a baker's dozen at one time in all fields—music, painting, sculpture, literature, oratory, philosophy, science."

Perhaps Sadakichi meant to speak of his own fate when he went on to say, "It is the cruel law of human existence that hundreds of men must drudge their whole lives away in order that one who is not a bit better than they may succeed. It is the same way in art: hundreds of talents must struggle and suffer in vain that one may reach the cloud-wrapped summit of popularity and fame. And that road is sure to lead over many corpses; and many of the nobler altruistic qualities of man have to be left far behind in the valley of unknown names."

On August 26 Sadakichi left by bus for Banning. He was growing impatient because I was working at the motion-picture studios instead of spending all my time with him. As he boarded the bus he shouted that Fowler was not the man to do his life story; probably was not big enough; couldn't get around to it; and threatened to look for some author who could keep awake.

In a letter to Barrymore, Hartmann had this to say: "Gene Fowler sleeps most of his time on earth. I do not quite see how you can claim to know him. Whenever he comes to Decker's studio the bed is 'temporarily permanently' occupied. Even Decker with his funny little mustachio has no chance to cope with Fowler's flophouse tendencies. It takes

a lot of leisure to write halfway beautifully! Einstein denies
'Time.' Fowler actually has no time; he has to jot down whatever comes to him as soon as he awakens."

On the night of August 28 Sadakichi unexpectedly reappeared at the Bundy Drive studio just as the Deckers, Barrymore, and I were about to sit down to a late dinner. He took
his accustomed place at the head of the table and prepared
to carve the roast of beef.

The old man had some difficulty in slicing the meat.
"Dull!" he said of the knife. "Like the company I'm in."

After dinner he delivered a lecture on the iniquities of
German philosophy. He also said that German music, as well
as Russian, should be barred from the air waves. "That
would leave to America only the Negro spirituals and jazz;
both forms much too good for the stupid public."

Toward the end of his lecture he lapsed into German and
concluded in French. I pointed out to him that none of us,
except Decker, understood German and only Barrymore had
an inkling of French.

"What's the difference?" he said. "You also don't understand English."

Barrymore asked Sadakichi to tell us what he considered
the most beautiful words in the English language. "There
are only two such words," he replied, "neither of them precisely English. The words most beautiful to me are Sadakichi Hartmann. I never tire of hearing them."

"Did you know," Decker said, "that Douglas Fairbanks
once referred to you as 'an intelligent spittoon'?"

"You are raking up this slander," Sadakichi retorted,

"merely because I will not fawn over your own work. Thank you very much."

Before Sadakichi had an opportunity to enlarge upon this subject W. C. Fields' housekeeper telephoned to inform us that the comedian had gone to Soboba Springs for treatment of his swollen ankles.

Hartmann had this to say of drinking men: "If you want to drink, you should do it. If you care more about drinking than you do for your work or your health, then by all means you should drink. But you never should make any apologies for your excesses, and no trips to the sanitariums. Just drink, and die, and leave the rest to the angels. Hah!"

---

EIGHT

*If all year round
With blossoms the hills were white,
Would they seem as bright?*
—Sadakichi

Dave Chasen, a graduate of the Broadway theater of comedian Joe Cook's day, and now a restaurant owner in Beverly Hills, received an airplane shipment of turbot one Saturday afternoon. After the customers had gone home he decided to stay in his large kitchen to cook one of the fish, and early the next morning, with the baked turbot in a silver-covered vessel, he and I set out to see W. C. Fields at Soboba Springs, a health resort eighty-four miles southeast of Los Angeles. Former heavyweight champion James J. Jeffries used to bathe in its mineral waters while preparing for his California fights. Some years ago Big Jim had persuaded his friend Fields to boil out at Soboba from time to time.

Fields greeted us warmly, and we could see that he was pleased, for the toothpick at the corner of his mouth moved up and down. He often was to be seen, at home or abroad, with a toothpick in his mouth. He used toothpicks not only to preserve his small, even teeth, but also as a means to break himself of the cigarette habit. When offended—and that was most of the time—Fields would retract the toothpick halfway inside his mouth and hold it motionless, like a readied stinger. When pleased, he would make the toothpick twitch like a seal's whisker.

"Ah!" W. C. exclaimed as Chasen set down the silver-lidded dish. "What's in it? The head of John the Baptist?"

"Turbot," said Chasen. "Baked turbot, English style."

The comedian, who said he came of a long line of starved costermongers, liked English cooking. "I am without bottles up here," he said. "May I offer you a slug of the local cathartic?"

"No thanks," Chasen said. The restaurant man was looking at perhaps twenty bankbooks spread out upon a card table. "Are you hunting for a shortage in your accounts?"

"A man who has been stranded as many times as me, and in faraway places, has to look out for his pennies," said Fields, shuffling the bankbooks as if to deal a hand of cards. "These little ledgers represent some of my backlog. Deposits in all the larger cities. Confidentially, I have the equivalent of ten thousand dollars in a Berlin bank."

"You're kidding!" said Chasen.

"Or else you're nuts," I said. "With the war on, and the inflation in Germany, how do you expect to get your dough from Hitler?"

He put on a superior expression, and the toothpick stopped moving. "Suppose the little bastard *wins?*"

Some years afterward, when his will was probated, Fields'

estate was appraised at almost eight hundred thousand dollars. In a conversation I had with his closest friend, Gregory LaCava, after the terms of the will had been made known, Greg said, "I know damned well that Bill had a great deal more money than appears on the surface. First of all, he had made millions, and kept most of it. He told me he had safe-deposit boxes, under screwy names, all over the country; and I believed him. It was just like him to put away great chunks where no one but he could get at the loot. When he was through with life he just didn't want the people he disliked to enjoy his money."

At Soboba Springs that day Fields said, "I'd like to remember you good lads in my will, but you'd only give it away to your friends." He added, "It's not your friends who destroy you, it's your friends' friends." He thought for a time, then continued, "If I knew the day and the hour the Man in the Bright Nightgown was coming to get me, I'd put all my dough into bills of large denomination, stand beside it on a balcony, and summon my dear relatives to watch me as I tore it into little pieces and strewed it like confetti to the winds."

In a later conversation W. C. confided, "I'm leaving my money to a Philadelphia home for Negro orphans. The poor little devils need help; besides, it will drive some people I know off their rockers."

When the will was read certain reporters were amazed to learn that "only white orphans" were to share in his estate. This apparent show of race prejudice came about in a most Fieldsian way. After the United States had entered the war, and there was a shortage of household help, one of W. C.'s Negro servants seemed, in his eyes, to be taking advantage of the situation.

"Just for that"—and he spoke with some heat—"I'm changing my will. No colored orphans!"

"That's a mistake," I told him. "Such a narrow gesture will make you misunderstood and much disliked."

"I've always been misunderstood," he rasped. "Besides, did you ever hear of a corpse complaining of unpopularity?"

To interpret the biased opinions of this doughty man would strain the faculties of any master of case histories. Is it not possible that the comedian's knockabout days as a hungry, roving child had much to do with his severe indictments of humanity?

If I were to apologize for W. C. Fields, or for any other member of our group for that matter, or attempt to justify his or their wayward actions, their shades would cry out with indignation. False praise is the province of the epitaph-maker and is best done with a chisel on a stone seldom visited. I needed no pretext to like these men, nor they me. They were not hypocrites; they never changed character; and at bottom they were men, every one of them, to the end. And as I looked on—or rather, participated—it became quite clear to me, if not to the men themselves, that they were severally enacting the final scenes of a tragedy—no matter the comic masks they wore. Each in his own fashion had lived too much in conflict with his God-given talents, as well as against the world of thou-shalt-not; and so they now must walk in the long shadow; but never for outsiders to see them except in their caps and bells. They were their own executioners.

On the day Chasen and I called at Soboba Springs, Uncle Claude berated me for continuing to subsidize Sadakichi Hartmann. "You are contributing to senile delinquency," he said. "You stake him and he knocks you. When you help one bum a lot of others see a sucker and put the bite on you. It's always that way, and you'll die broke. This here Itchy-Scratchy of yours is even mooching on the government, on *my* taxes, and living free on an Indian reservation."

This reminded our host that an Indian reservation was situated not far away from Soboba Springs. He proposed that we drive over at once to learn how his taxes were being misspent. Despite the heat of the day W. C. put on a robe over his sunbather's trunks—the fluffy white robe with the huge bunch of keys and the fat roll of currency in the respective side pockets, and a fresh supply of toothpicks.

The reservation seemed even more run-down than the one upon which Sadakichi lived. Fields pointed out the recreation grounds, where several half-naked young Indians were tossing a scuffed basketball. "God forgive the Great White Father!" he exclaimed, and called our attention to the patch of flints and stones and the rusted chicken-wire goal-baskets stapled to rickety poles. "Lazarus used to play here," he said.

"Those papooses"—the irate taxpayer lost his toothpick as he continued speaking—"won't even be allowed to drink booze when they grow up. All we ever gave the Indians were our choice diseases and a lot of broken treaties." He glared in the general direction of Washington, D. C. "Isn't it wonderful what we are doing *to* the Indians?"

Back at the spa we said good-by to Uncle Claude, who again offered us a drink of the Soboba waters "for the road." He stood on the porch of his bungalow, a fresh toothpick wigwagging at the corner of his mouth, and watched us get into the car.

As Chasen and I drove toward Los Angeles we did not speak for a long time. Dave smoked his pipe till it went out, then finally said, "I have a hunch that the old boy really puts on a lot of his crabbiness just to hide a soft spot in his character. What do you think?"

"Bill is a lonely man," I replied. "And, for that matter, who isn't? The only difference between him and the rest of us in that respect is that we sing out against Fate as a group, a kind of glee club, while Fields is a soloist, and a mighty audible one. He's been caught napping a few times though; for instance, when I was thought to be dying the night I turned over in McCarey's car. Bill's butler later told me that Fields locked the door to his bedroom and said he would answer the telephone only if the hospital called. He was heard crying out several times. He kept his lights burning till dawn. Next day, however, he sent me such insulting telephone messages that the nurse hesitated to relay them, fearing a relapse."

"Like the time," Chasen said, "when Billy Grady, his old-time manager, told me in his presence that Uncle Claude liked flowers, 'You keep your Irish-Catholic mouth shut!' he yelled at Grady."

"Yes," I said. "I once asked W. C. why he didn't like dogs.

'Because,' he answered, 'the sons-of-bitches—and they really are, you know—lift their legs on flowers.' "

Uncle Claude was the most ornery lovable man I have ever known. He hid none of his faults from the world; indeed, he hid nothing except perhaps some of his money, and most of his good deeds, which were more numerous than might be imagined.

NINE

Tell me, autumn night,
What is perturbing my mind?
Is it that I wait
For one who does not come?
Or is it the moan of the wind?
                    —Sadakichi

I returned from Soboba Springs to find only the candles burning at the Bundy Drive studio. A man from the utilities company had turned off the electricity and gas that afternoon.

"Why don't you pay the bill?" I asked Decker. "You surely have something left over from the sale of the Venetian picture."

The artist was receiving much better pay for his work than in other days when, with an assortment of sketches and paintings stacked against the back seat of his battered car, he had made catch-as-catch-can tours of Beverly Hills and Pasadena.

One of America's wealthiest young women, while at a social get-together at the house of Decker's good friend Paulette Goddard, chanced to mention that she had known her most happy years as a girl in Venice. She complained that artists nowadays seldom painted anything Venetian except cliché scenes of St. Mark's, or of the Square, the Doges' Palace, the Bridge of Sighs, gondolas on the Grand Canal, and the like.

"It so happens that I have just finished a Venetian picture," Decker hastened to say. "An off-beat view of Lord Byron's residence. I too detest such pot-boiler work as you have described."

"May I see the picture?"

"Of course. When would you like?'

"Right now."

Decker had not yet painted the work, except in his mind's eye. "I promised to call on Judge Alfred Paonessa," he sparred. "But I'll be back at my studio in, say, three hours."

During the dashaway for home and paint pots the artist got a ticket—for speeding, going through a red traffic signal, and driving without a license. He lost half an hour in the traffic officer's company, then got home and to work at his easel. He blurred the façade of Lord Byron's house because of his haste in overlaying fresh paints. He always painted rapidly, and would wait for a day at most till the surface became, as he called it, tacky, before going on with a picture. To facilitate matters he usually mixed a quick-drying varnish with the paints—a bad practice indeed, if events such as the cracking or chipping of a brittle surface are to be forestalled. Decker knew all this, of course, but frequent hardship and hunger, and an impatient desire to lose himself in successive creations, made speed almost an obsession with him. He painted mostly on plywood board instead of canvas, I think, because the elasticity of stretched canvas might spring loose the prematurely dry medium. It is only fair, however, to give his own reason for painting upon board; he said that he was most vigorous of hand and liked to feel a solid resistance, as of a shield against the thrusts, as he attacked the board with the brush.

When the heiress arrived at the studio Decker explained that he had been retouching the work here and there. "It's exactly what I want," said the wealthy young woman. "I'll have a check for twenty-five hundred dollars mailed to you immediately."

Decker had no use for banks, where one's deposits might be attached by creditors. As soon as he received his check for the Venetian work he cashed it in the form of fifty-dollar bills, then hid the banknotes, as was his custom, in a supposedly authentic pirate's chest that he kept in a tiny dirt cellar beneath the floorboards of a clothes closet.

Whenever he needed money—which was all the time—he would descend, as though into the shaft of a mine, unlock the pirate's chest, and soon again pop up with money and sly smiles. The artist kept no account of his fluctuating treasures. If he found the mother lode had been played out, he would come from below with the cry, "It's gone! All gone!"

Tonight was just such an occasion of bankruptcy. He had come up empty-handed from the burrow, twisted his mustache, thought things over, then saw something on Sadakichi's shoe soles that caused him to ask, "How did that brown earth get on your boots, eh?"

"I was walking in the garden," Hartmann replied in an aloof manner and turned to Barrymore, who was hiding behind a newspaper (a trick he sometimes employed to ensure privacy), to say, "Santayana is a philosopher without coherence. And as for John Dewey, I am constantly confusing him with the man who fought the naval engagement at Manila."

Still gazing at the soles of Sadakichi's congressional boots, Decker pretended to be concerned as to how W. C. Fields was faring at Soboba. Without waiting for me to tell him of my visit, Decker moved closer to Hartmann's chair with the observation, "The dirt floor in the cellar is light brown adobe. There is light brown wet clay on your soles—unless I am as color blind as Paul Gustave Doré."

Sadakichi waved scornfully. "California is made of adobe, and so are its inhabitants."

Hartmann's secretary now arrived with her stenographer's notebook and pen. After Decker let her in the door he seemed to forget his suspicions of Sadakichi and at his darkened easel began to rail at the gas and electric company, bemoaning the lack of proper light for his painting and gas for cooking.

Barrymore still was pretending to read by the dim candlelight. Phyllis Decker had gone to the kitchen to comfort a cocker spaniel that was about to become a mother, by the light of a kerosene-burning red lantern that someone must have stolen from a street-repair project.

Sadakichi was dictating: "The Belt of Orion rises to the rhythmic beat of one-two-three, in a celestial waltz. That is where the concept came of the 'music of the spheres.' Sometimes you don't recognize the same constellations; for certain stars dance, influenced by vibrations of our atmosphere.

Men who sleep in the open have a little bit of the idea. We have too many ceilings. I would abolish all ceilings. In fact" —he was referring to the windstorm that had raised his Banning roof—"Nature helped me abolish one of mine."

Meanwhile Decker kept on complaining, to this effect: "The finance company is trying to get my car. Dammit! I spend what I get for paints and materials, including brandy. The gas people sent over a crude bastard this afternoon. A loud oaf. I said I'd pay the bill when I got damned good and ready, and he called me a deadbeat, then turned everything off. But what infuriated me most was that he sneered at my painting. You know, the one over there. The hornplayer. I've decided to call it 'The Man Next Door.' I'll get even!"

Sadakichi, having listened to Decker with half an ear, remarked that artists should let time and circumstance take care of their minor revenges. He cited two instances to prove his statement. When the proprietor of Luchow's Restaurant had barred him from the Fourteenth-Street premises for having thrown clamshells at the string orchestra (Hartmann detested Strauss waltzes) the restaurant owner collapsed with appendicitis, as though hexed, and went to the hospital. At another time, Sadakichi recalled, a pickpocket stole from him a necklace, which Hartmann had "borrowed" while dancing with a Greenwich Village tourist. "I simply was a more skillful pickpocket than he, and promptly recovered and displayed it to everyone. The pickpocket lost face among his colleagues. Hah!"

"Things do catch up with people," Decker agreed. He turned to Sadakichi's secretary. "You can make notes of this too. I once had a girl who left me for a Chinese gambler. I thought I'd visit this Oriental poacher merely to see what kind of a fan-tan dealer was beating my time. I sat waiting for an hour in a taxicab in front of his house; just curious, you know. I popped out of the cab when he came out the front door of his place. He evidently thought I was going to shoot him, for I'll be damned if he didn't drop dead right at my feet!"

Barrymore peeked from behind his newspaper (as I recall it, he had been pretending to study the want-ad section). "Did you get the girl back?"

"No, but I sold the picture I had painted of her to a bootlegger, the gambler's successor. After looking at her true character, as painted by me, he promptly gave her the air."

Sadakichi continued his dictation, page upon page; he spoke of his early loves, of his life in the art capitals of Europe, and expressed his views upon anything and everything, including his definition of the Sunday newspaper, an institution which was, he declared, a preparatory school for the insane asylum.

I have before me as I write almost three thousand pages of Sadakichiana: the transcriptions made by Hartmann's secretaries, a reference file of his writings and recorded opinions, as well as my own notes taken at the last meetings in Bundy Drive or set down while memory was fresh.

It may be correctly charged that all this was a waste of effort. Indeed, W. C. Fields remarked of these activities, "Mr. William R. Hearst hit the nail squarely on the head the time he said you were like the fellow who winked at his sweetheart in the dark: *he* knew what he was doing; but nobody *else* did."

That night Hartmann rolled off a list of fifty-two addresses at which he had lived in America and in Europe before he moved to California. His roster of hosts here and abroad was a catalogue of writers, artists, and musicians of the 1880s and the 1890s. To gain entrance to the salons and studios, he had represented himself not only as a friend of Walt Whitman, but also as a correspondent for the *New York Staats-Zeitung* and the *New York Herald*. He had been, in fact, a free-lance contributor to these and other newspapers; and had sold stories and articles to various national magazines and art periodicals. He had also delivered lectures, or given readings from the works of his literary acquaintances, and passed the hat.

He remembered with great relish his times at Mallarmé's salon in Paris, and his several visits to Paul Heyse's house in Munich. It would seem that Mallarmé had been the most durable of his hosts. Heyse, as had Whitman, eventually found it necessary to disown one of Hartmann's interviews. Sadakichi represented him as having assailed Ibsen's then-daring discussions of human relationships and quoted Heyse as having said: "Ibsen has ceased to be a poet. A great pity! He was such a superb romanticist in *Brand* and *Peer Gynt*."

An anxious Hartmann, it would appear, never quite managed to charm the great Ibsen. "I saw him every afternoon as I went to the theater in Munich. He would sit at the Maximilian Café, reading the papers or looking over his spectacles at the people passing by. His *Wild Duck* had just appeared. Several times I sought to converse with him, but he would only grunt and look away. Alas! Had he but known that I was to be his most zealous American pioneer —but all too early for my New England lecture-audiences— he would have disclosed to me his innermost secrets."

In Paris, Sadakichi said, Debussy behaved like a snob. "The most effective thing he had done as a musician—and he was then but a comer-upper—had been to manage eloquent periods of silence in his compositions. Judicious silences are important in any work—musical, or in moments of love."

At this pronouncement Jack Barrymore, who for some time had been in the kitchen acting as midwife's assistant, returned to the main room for a glass of wine. He was carrying the red lantern in brakeman's fashion, to warn all traffic out of his way.

"Instead of writing a book on Sadakichi," said Barrymore, winking, as he poured himself a vermouth, "we should commission Gutzon Borglum to carve a likeness of him upon Mount Rushmore."

"Gutzon Borglum," Hartmann exploded, "is the hillbilly of sculptors! The only useful thing that will come out of this damnable war in Europe is that Borglum will be compelled to stay away from the Alps." He waved his long arms. "I am about to describe a romance or two. My loves, Barrymore, were far greater and deeper than yours, though not so widely publicized. Did you ever see the beautiful Sadie Malreaux? Or were you ever loved by her?"

"You are confusing me with my late father." Jack downed his drink. "He knew the lady you just mentioned, but of course he was too much of a gentleman to confide the details to more than the entire membership of the Lambs Club."

Barrymore, swinging his lantern happily, went back to the kitchen to resume his obstetrical duties on behalf of the puppies.

Decker was saying, as though to himself, "I'll get even with that gas-company dolt if it's the last thing I do!" He interrupted his soliloquy to ask Sadakichi, "Wasn't Sadie the dame who caused you to try to knock yourself off?"

Hartmann delivered a tirade in German. The secretary asked if he would please translate anything that was important.

"Everything I say is important, young lady! You may record my prediction that Decker will end his life painting barns." The old fellow rose to go to the bathroom. At the door he paused to make further prophecies. "And Barrymore will die in the gutter. And Fowler will break his neck while stumbling over a dictionary in his sleep."

Barrymore reappeared from the kitchen for another bracer. "Six puppies so far," he announced. "The mother is doing fine. And so am I."

Behind the bathroom door Sadakichi began to swear, and we heard the crash of glass.

"It's his truss," said Barrymore.

"Decker," I said, "it's dangerous to have no light on in the bathroom. We'll pay that bill first thing tomorrow."

"Why do you keep a toothbrush holder on a toilet seat?" Sadakichi shouted, emerging.

He sat down and resumed his dictation. "When a missionary is among cannibals he must be prepared to take pot-luck." Then he asked his secretary, "Before I begin an outline of the true order of things, would you consider a proposal of marriage?" He got no encouragement, so continued, "No sex whatsoever. You would be free to have lovers while we traveled first class all over Europe. But of course you would be required to admire my mind at all times. Does that appeal to you, young woman?"

"No."

"Thank you very much. Now let us treat of a more civilized time."

By 1892 he had made three voyages to Europe. During his second visit, in 1888, he went from Holland to London in an all but penniless state. On his first day in London he called, in turn, upon William Michael Rossetti and William Morris. He invested his last shillings to rent a Prince Albert coat, a pair of gray gloves, and a walking stick. He placed a sprig of parsley in his lapel, merely to show that he was no ordinary boulevardier.

"I hoped to obtain from these men an introduction to Laureate Tennyson," Sadakichi recalled. "And perhaps a crust of bread."

" 'Why do you wish to see Lord Tennyson?' Rossetti asked. 'Because I'm starving,' I replied. Rossetti had some tea things brought in; and I might have gained his financial favor were it not for my honesty in matters of artistic opinion. I would not overpraise the paintings of his late brother Dante Gabriel; and when I remarked that I considered *The Blessed Damozel* much inferior to Poe's *Raven*—yearning in reverse, from Heaven to Earth—he chilled. Almost the same thing happened a few hours later on my visit to William Morris. I said the furniture he was making belonged to the tomb of Hadrian. He frowned when I removed the parsley from my lapel and proceeded to eat the vegetable."

Sadakichi then launched into a long description of his days as a social lion in Boston. He had given lectures in that city on Ibsen and contributed art comments to the local newspapers. It was while he was living there that he had tried to form his Whitman Club, and in so doing met Lowell, Whittier, Emerson, and several other literary factotums.

Barrymore returned for a third vermouth. "We have a seventh puppy," he announced. "I am the Dr. Dafoe of dogs."

"And now," Sadakichi said, "I shall dictate, for all posterity to learn, how a frustrated love can overwhelm young genius. I went from Boston to New York, lived a nomadic life, taught elocution, and worshiped women as if they were supernatural creatures—"

"As indeed they *are*," Barrymore interrupted archly.

"No stupid asides, if you please. My imagination," Sadakichi went on, "freed them from all earthiness."

"Sadakichi," Decker interjected, "is an even greater man than himself."

"I had given several lectures in the Adirondacks," the old fellow continued, "the summer resorts. Very little cash was put in the collection plate, and sometimes I had to leave without paying for my board and lodgings."

In New York, from 1889 until 1891, he sustained himself by writing occasional columns for the *Herald* and the *Phil-*

adelphia Times, and by acting as a guide for young women
visitors to the museum. Sometimes he would manage to sell
an art essay. During this lean period he developed a rupture
while struggling for breath during a midnight attack of
asthma.

He decided to give elocution lessons, and took a room in
a cheap boarding house. But just one pupil answered his ad
in the personal column of the *Herald.* Genevieve, a girl of
sixteen, accompanied by an ambitious mother of moderate
means, applied for a course in Delsarte. Sadakichi fell in
love with the girl. Though her mother pointed out that he
was ten years older than his student and that the lass knew
little of the world, despite the fact that she had been a roller-
skating performer in Hell's Kitchen, Hartmann became so
infatuated that he decided to give her lessons free of charge.

Once Sadakichi called upon the family at their flat on
Tenth Avenue. The dinginess of the place oppressed him.
"Everything in the parlor was in bad taste. Particularly offensive to me were two clumsy china dogs on the mantelpiece. I was put in a strangely despondent mood; rather, a
kind of hallucination that made all objects around me look
too small, stunted, under life-size, as it were; as though I
had strayed into some Lilliput and found myself too large
for the dimensions of the room."

Genevieve's father, Sadakichi went on to say, came shuffling into the parlor. He was a short, heavily built, common-
place sort of man with a black mustache, employed as a
nightwatchman at a Paterson, New Jersey, silk mill. He
strongly disapproved of the lessons.

"Just forget about my daughter," the father said emphatically. "My wife is just a plain damn fool to put ideas about the stage in her head."

The father's strong objections made no impression on the mother, who arranged for Sadakichi to meet her daughter in secret on nights the watchman was away at work; she sometimes paid for gallery seats at the theater. Eventually the father became aware of these trysts and moved his family to Paterson.

Sadakichi visited the New Jersey silk town whenever he could save enough fare. The girl's older brother, a bartender built like Sandow the Strong Man, called upon Hartmann at the boarding house. He threatened to flatten him with a bungstarter if he so much as spoke again to the kid sister.

"Alone in my lodgings," Sadakichi said, "I felt as though the earth had swallowed me. I took off my coat, pushed up my shirtsleeves, smashed a drinking glass, and cut my left wrist and forearm with the shards—once, twice, half a dozen times, always deeper and deeper; and at last I succeeded in piercing a vein. I staggered about the room, posed as if I were dying, and finally called the landlord. That old, gray-bearded gentleman had felt exceedingly friendly toward me ever since I had accidentally discovered him with a servant girl on his lap and had kept silent about it. He tied my arm with a handkerchief, brought me a glass of wine, and called a doctor."

Sadakichi's left arm was in a sling next day when he went to the Café Manhattan to ask for a free meal. When he returned to the boarding house the door of his room was locked against him. The landlord pointed out that Hartmann already owed him one hundred and thirty dollars for room rent, but gave the young man a ten and permission to take his personal belongings with him.

The landlord's wife, however, insisted that Sadakichi return a borrowed volume of Shakespeare before allowing him to gather up his few possessions. "Unfortunately," Sadakichi said, "I had sold this book for seventy-five cents. I ran to the bookstore in the hope of buying it back, but it had been resold."

Somehow he persuaded the landlord's wife to surrender his valise, but she would not return his overcoat. "I wandered to Eighth Street," he said, "where I found a garret over a costumer's establishment. My room, if such it could be called, adjoined that of a young musician. What I did in the following days I do not remember clearly. I was utterly reckless, and one night found myself almost mad because of my evil luck and my sorrow over Genevieve. I threatened to set the place on fire. I made one scene after another, knocked my head against the wall, upset the furniture, cursed fate, the entire world, and all its inhabitants. The young musician became frightened, and soon I heard voices. People came upstairs—the landlord in his dressing gown, his wife holding a candle, and, back of them, a policeman. I lay in bed and feigned delirium. The policeman shook me, then said, 'He's all right, but if anything happens, call me.'"

In a few days Sadakichi managed somehow to arrange an appointment with Genevieve and her mother at the Café Manhattan. He soon found that the mother and daughter no longer were dazzled by his talents. The elder woman said there were to be no more meetings. When he turned to the girl, she made light of the wounds he had inflicted upon himself. Thereupon the love-mad fellow dashed out-of-doors and wandered off in the late-autumn rain that was veiling the town.

The next thing he clearly remembered was finding himself on a park bench in Union Square. It was very late, and, except for an occasional policeman cowled and coated against the weather, few persons passed by. The street lamps flickered, and the cold rain dripped from the branches of the almost leafless trees.

Hartmann said that he heard an inner voice, the sepulchral voice that so many anguished drifters hear, and always will hear, as they sit forlorn and hungry and wet on New York's park benches: "What next? What next?"

A woman of the streets took pity on him. She guided him to her own miserable room in a flat near the East River. The outcasts fell asleep, forgetful for a little time of the coldness and the indifference of the world.

TEN

In the gardens the asters fade;
Smoke of fire-weeds blurs the plain.
The hours pass with a sullen grace.
　　　　　　　　　—Sadakichi

Decker paid his gas- and electric-light bill, and also got even with the fellow who had turned off the studio utilities, who had called him a deadbeat and then sneered at the painting of the man with the trombone.

"I don't like critics of any sort," Decker said. "With but few exceptions they are the back-seat drivers of the arts."

Mr. Decker, cash in hand and nattily attired, and with gold ornaments clanking at his wrists, insisted upon paying his bill to someone in authority at the utilities branch office. A deputy responded.

"I have been in New York for three months," Decker boldly falsified. "By some oversight my business agent neglected to take care of this bill."

The official understood this kind of thing perfectly and smiled as he stamped the receipt.

"Are all your men," Decker asked with simulated con-

cern, "as disloyal as the guy who turned off my gas and electricity?"

"I beg your pardon?"

Decker pretended regret at having said what he had. "I
should have kept my mouth shut. Thank you and good
day."

"Just a moment," said the man. "Did he speak out of
turn?"

"Forget it," said Decker self-righteously. "I guess some
people get a kick out of knocking their bosses."

"What? What's this?"

"Your courtesy to me," the artist said, "is a complete denial of everything he said."

"Tell me, if you please, exactly what happened."

"Not with those ladies at the counter."

The man leaned halfway across the barrier to say in a low
voice, "Would you give me just a sample of it?"

Decker also lowered his voice. "This guy described your
manager as a complete horse's ass and said if the big shots
downtown knew how all of you lay down on the job you'd
be sacked."

The official paled at these words of treason. "Mr. Decker,
I want to thank you for reporting this."

With his electric lights aglow once again, and the oven-
burners as hot as the dice of Nick the Greek, Decker resumed his painting and his cooking. There was an excellent
dinner of stuffed ox-heart that evening, with red cabbage
cooked in Moselle wine, little pork sausages, potatoes Anna,
and English trifle.

The trifle was served on a set of handsome antique plates

borrowed by Decker from an ever-helpful next-door neighbor—the only neighbor who never complained about night
noises, Mrs. Harriet deLaix. It was, I thought, the only
flaw in the dinner. I did not like trifle at Decker's; I do
not like it in England; nor would I like it even in France,
where, I believe, the mere mention of trifle is punishable
by a one-way journey to the Iron Widow.

Roland J. McKinney, then the director of art at the Los
Angeles Museum of History, Science, and Art, dined at
Decker's studio that night. Others at the board were Jack
Barrymore, whose lawyer had permitted him to supply the
food from his weekly allowance of one hundred dollars; I,
who had underwritten the wine; and Sadakichi, who contributed Sadakichi. Hartmann of course sat at the head of
the table, a carving knife poised over the stuffed and spiced
ox-heart.

McKinney happened to say that he had studied in the
same art group as his friend the late George Wesley Bellows. That artist's paintings and lithographs of prizefighters
had impressed me profoundly. Although, as a former box-
ing reporter, it had been apparent to me that Bellows' pugilists assumed impractical stances—were so wide-winged and
open they would have had their blocks knocked off by good
counter-punchers—the very smell of stale tobacco smoke
and rosin dust; the stench of hair tonic and cheap cologne
that gamblers and managers thought as socially necessary as
their yellow diamonds; the sweating, stripped athletes whose
courage rang out above the gong sound that summoned
them to battle—a rhythmic violence that faded from the
game with the retirement of Jack Dempsey, Harry Greb,

and Mickey Walker, and, except for Joe Louis, Henry Armstrong, and Sugar Ray Robinson, gave way to mere circus acrobatics—all these strong accents of the older-day arenas seemed present and alive in Bellows' pictorial memoirs of ringside and gymnasium. He was the Pierce Egan of artists, painting instead of writing his *Boxiana*.

When I said as much at table Sadakichi snarled, "Fowler's opinions on art should be suppressed by the Humane Society. He even thinks Decker is a great painter." He turned to McKinney. "I'll have you remember that as early as 1910 I predicted that Bellows would become important. When he quit imitating Goya and Daumier and turned his back on black and white emphasis, he discovered the pageantry of color and so attained distinction."

McKinney nodded in agreement. "I have managed to acquire a fine Bellows for the museum; not a prize-fighting study, however. It demonstrates what you say of his handling of color."

McKinney recommended that we visit the museum, not only to inspect the Bellows but also to see forty-two masterpieces that originally had been on display respectively at the New York and San Francisco World's Fairs. These old masters, which had been lent to the American expositions by various European museums and private collectors before the outbreak of World War II, now could not be returned to their owners. They were to be on view at the Los Angeles Museum until September 15.

"I should think," McKinney said to Sadakichi, "that you of all persons would come down to see these pictures."

"Fourth- and fifth-rate," Sadakichi replied.

McKinney smiled. "I wouldn't say that."

"Well, I would," was Sadakichi's retort.

McKinney said that a curator's life was not easy; he had to be a politician as well as an expert on art. To get something as trivial as a new pencil he had to fill out a requisition in duplicate. Someone remarked that art lovers should vote for county officials who could tell the difference between a Velázquez and a sack of oats.

McKinney said to Barrymore, "I hope you will vote for someone who understands art."

"I vote for no one," said Jack.

"You don't vote?" Roland asked.

"Never."

"Why not?"

Barrymore speared a piece of ox-heart with his fork. "Because Abraham Lincoln is not running for office."

The next day I volunteered to take Sadakichi to the museum. The sun of late July beat down like a scourge. When I got behind the wheel of my convertible it was like sitting on the Village Blacksmith's forge. But Sadakichi seemed never to have enough heat; he had on his gray woolen overcoat, a bright green muffler, and the same old felt hat.

At the entrance to the museum Hartmann spied a wheelchair. Without a word he sat down in it and motioned for me to trundle him inside the exhibition hall. There were perhaps three hundred persons in the gallery, some of them earnestly consulting brown paper-bound catalogues, others strolling about or standing in reverent groups as though waiting for the undertaker to bring in the body of a rich aunt.

Several gallery visitors glanced at the hatted and over-coated old fellow in the wheelchair, then returned to their mortuary-chapel behavior. When, however, Hartmann's baritone lanced through the silence with, "They must be dedicating an aspirin tablet here!" the persons nearest us showed displeasure.

I suppose I looked like an Atlantic City boardwalk man as I chaired the old critic up to Jan van Eyck's "Virgin and Child" (the Ince Hall Madonna). He examined this small panel closely. "Painted it on his day off!" he exclaimed.

A few museum visitors were gathering near the chair, and someone asked, "Who is this strange old man?" Sadakichi raised a hand and called out, "I am a voice crying in the wilderness."

In turn, I wheeled the critic in front of Dürer's "Portrait of a Woman," El Greco's "The Deposition," and Frans Hals' small "Portrait of Hendrik Swalmius"; we then stopped before a group of four Rembrandts, one of them a self-portrait painted in 1662. That self-portrait stirred Sadakichi's vocal protest. "Spurious!" he called out. "Spurious!" A museum attendant requested that he keep his voice down. To which Sadakichi replied, "Then keep your fakeries down!"

One spectator out of the twenty or so persons now following us from place to place, a spunky woman in rimless eyeglasses and a suit of some dark material, protested to Sadakichi, "This is a genuine Rembrandt. And you could at least take off your hat."

Without turning his head he replied, "Madam, why don't you spend your time at a sideshow? You seem to be fond of freaks!"

Expert opinion holds that the panel is a genuine Rembrandt; but at the time of Hartmann's attack upon it he pointed out that the catalogue bore the words: "Signed on the right at top by a later hand."

When he dismissed the portrait of Rembrandt's wife Saskia as "second rate," the same lady asked, "But you admit that *this* is an authentic work?"

"I do," and Sadakichi motioned for me to wheel him elsewhere. "But he had begun to lose his mind when he painted it."

Hartmann had a good word or two for Vermeer's "The Milkmaid" and for three or four other paintings; but mostly he expressed adverse criticism, in varying degrees of intensity: of Willem Kalf's "Still Life with Nautilus Cup"—"What everybody can do"; of Jan Steen's "The Twelfth-Night Feast"—"Too hard"; and of Adriaen van Ostade's "Woman Selling Fish"—"I hope that she will sell them."

We paused before Turner's "Burial at Sea of Sir David Wilkie." The relatively large group that now surrounded the chair to hear the cantankerous old man—a few of them apparently delighted with his words of dissent, but the others frowning—were unprepared for the next words and gestures. Half rising from the chair, Hartmann doffed his hat to the Turner and in a loud voice called out, "Bravo! Bravo!"

The minority gave Sadakichi a ripple of applause. Roland McKinney came out of his office to see if vandals were on the loose. When he discovered us he put a hand to his brow and seemed unable to speak.

"We are going now," I said into Roland's ear.

He managed to find his voice. "Oh, thank God!"

"Where is the washroom?" Hartmann asked the curator.

McKinney pointed toward one of the exits. "Past that door and to the left."

"Bring it to me!" shouted the old egotist.

I wheeled him, for his kidneys' sake, and for the sake of the museum floor, to the designated place.

Back at his hotel Sadakichi demanded that I pay him a fee for the museum trip because the experience had sapped his energy and all but ruined his love for the beautiful. I sent out for brandy and cigars; then he got down to business with his secretary, to dictate what he called "A Hospital Romance."

"Oh, I was so weary of everything," Sadakichi said in recollection of his personal history during the early 1890s. "Weary of the world, of my surroundings, even of the plaster casts I had scrimped to buy—beautiful specimens of remote periods of artistic endeavor."

He was violently ill, he persuaded himself, and could not sleep. The slashed wrist became infected. It appears that some of his forebears had endowed the German Hospital; so when Sadakichi identified himself as a descendant of the Hamburg coffee merchants he was accepted as a non-paying patient.

"I was ushered into a large ward. Put to bed, I became violent, shouted at the top of my voice, had weeping spells, tossed about, and threw myself half out of bed. It was genuine enough; a nervous breakdown. An intern told me to behave or he would put me in a strait jacket."

Through his nightmarish experience filtered the melodious voice of a woman. "Is this the new patient?"

It was the voice of a nurse, a young woman of fine features and of intelligent mind. Her name was Betty Walsh, but Hartmann called her "the Madonna." He referred to her that way during the nights she attended him, nights when she discussed art and literature with him, for she was a discriminating reader of good books and a museum-goer.

Sadakichi revealed his whole life and aspirations to the Madonna. When at last he was able to walk again, and the nurse was assigned to a ward elsewhere in the hospital, he would meet her secretly from time to time in an unheated washroom.

"But her warm and understanding nature made up for the cold environment of the washroom. The young doctor who had threatened me with the strait jacket was venomously jealous of me because of this woman. One day I took his watch while he was leaning over to listen to my chest, for I had nimble fingers. Later I threw the watch in the toilet bowl."

When called to the superintendent's office to explain his actions, Hartmann not only described what he had done to the intern's watch but also admitted that he had kept washroom trysts with the nurse. "You should heat your washrooms," he said. "People catch cold in them."

The Madonna left the hospital the day after Hartmann was requested to go. Then, against the advice of the hospital superintendent, as well as that of a lawyer-friend of her Philadelphia family, the young woman decided to accept Sadakichi's proposal of marriage.

The newly married Hartmanns lived in one shabby rooming house after another, on Second Avenue near East Thirty-first Street in New York, then in Philadelphia, and next in Boston. There the half-Japanese Sadakichi finally made a stir among the impressionable ladies, at literary teas or at his drawing-room lectures.

"She subsequently gave me five of my thirteen children," said Sadakichi. "I don't know how long we stayed married. I never kept track of such matters; for it is more important to remember how content you have been in wedlock than how long it lasted. But I shall say that this woman encouraged me to enter upon the most productive period of my life. The fact that I wandered away, neglected her many times, and even had a natural son by another woman, did not dull her loyalty to me. I am Sadakichi Hartmann. Hah!"

For some time before his marriage Sadakichi had been contemplating a drama based upon his own non-historic and non-Biblical concepts of the life of Our Lord. "I sat down one day in 1892 at eleven in the morning," he said, "and wrote, without food or drink, until six the next morning, and finished this work. However, it was not published until 1893, and then privately, in Boston."

The *Christ* came out in a limited edition of four hundred copies, and almost immediately the twenty-nine-year-old playwright was set upon by Boston censors. He had depicted Christ as having been enamored of Mary Magdalene.

Huneker wrote of this work: "It is the most daring of all decadent productions."

"The books were confiscated," Sadakichi said. "I was arrested and spent Christmas week of 1893 in Charles Street Jail Number Two. The worst food I ever ate. Robert Ingersoll came to the jail and offered to defend me free of charge, but took affront when I accused him of being merely a professional atheist. I said I was not an atheist, but more of a 'Plumed Knight' than Blaine, whom Ingersoll had nominated for the presidency in 1876."

While in the clink Sadakichi received several enthusiastic letters from persons of modern mind. Upon his release he decided to answer in person a note from a young actress, Sadie Malreaux (if we may use a fictitious name here). She had invited him to call upon her at the theater.

"The Gilbert and Sullivan operas were in great vogue," Hartmann said. "Sadie was playing a minor role in *Pinafore*. As I entered her dressing room I saw that she was wearing duck trousers as no other woman could wear them. She was but twenty, petite, brown-haired, and dark-complexioned. I was inclined to forget that I was a married man and just recently the father of a baby girl."

The day after this meeting Hartmann visited Sadie at her Boston apartment, which was "all done in fruit and flowers, like a fruit store." The actress told him she had expected the author of such a drama to be a much older man.

Miss Malreaux appeared one day at the Hartmann boarding house with presents for both Mrs. Hartmann and her infant daughter. "The beautiful young woman drove up,"

Hartmann said, "in a two-horse carriage, with an old doctor at the reins. He wore red sideburns, and looked like the late President Chester A. Arthur, and seemed quite the dandy."

Soon after this the young actress left Boston with the theatrical company to play a New York engagement. "We're artists," Sadie said in parting. "We'll meet again."

They did meet, but after long intervals, and then briefly, during the years that followed. "She wanted to become a great actress." Sadakichi seemed to be in a state of most pleasant recollection. "The next time I saw her, years later, was at the Madison Square Garden Theatre. On the roof, you know? The place where Harry Thaw shot Stanford White. The play was *The Turtle*, as I recall it. Sadie was marvelously costumed in an evening gown in Act Two. Her beauty was in full flower, and I kept my opera glasses on her every movement. She had a mole on her right arm. I had read in the newspapers that she now was married to a Cuban sugar-plantation millionaire; he once sent someone to Paris to write a play for her."

Several more years passed. Sadakichi wrote his Whitman pamphlet, a drama entitled *Buddha* (described by critic Vance Thompson as "Something as gilded and monstrous and uncouth as the Temple of Benares"), and a dramatic episode, *A Tragedy in a New York Flat* (of which Edmund Clarence Stedman wrote, "Few can make a longer play, and have it as powerful in construction and dramatic truth").

Between literary occupations Hartmann worked as a filing clerk for the architectural firm of McKim, Mead, and White,

but got the sack for describing Stanford White's drawings
as "Rococo *in excelsis*. To be improved upon only by the
pigeons, after the drawings become buildings."

"I was King of Bohemia now," he said, "and had begun
my drama *Mohammed.* Sadie saw me on the street one day,
ordered her coachman to stop the carriage, and asked me to
ride with her in Central Park. She was still very beautiful,
forthright, and unrepressed."

"'Would you come to my house tonight?' she asked. She
gave me an address on Fifth Avenue, where the brownstone
mansions of those days stood as monuments to the heavy
Victorian taste of merchant princes and steel masters in the
selection of stone cocoons for their wives.

"'Coquelin, the French comedian, will be there,' Sadie
said, 'but only for dinner. I want to talk to you alone.'

"'What of your husband? The Cuban?'

"'I am giving it all up and going into vaudeville.' She
named as her partner a famous actor known for his unstable
temperament and wild jealousies."

At dinner that evening the conversation was carried on
mostly in French. After Coquelin left, Sadakichi "felt almost
in love." While making up his mind as to the proper strategy
he heard a man's voice from the reception hall. It was
Sadie's prospective vaudeville partner, calling unannounced.
She said he sometimes carried a pistol.

Sadakichi went out by way of the tradesmen's door.

After another silence of years, during which Sadakichi
produced his two most successful books, *History of American Art* (1901) and *Japanese Art* (1903), he again met

Sadie. He saw few changes in her, although she seemed more plump and somewhat weary.

" 'What have you done with yourself?' I asked her.

" 'I am living with an old man. He's rich.'

" 'Do you need any pictures? I'm doing some wonderful pastels.'

" 'Come to my apartment tonight and we'll see. The old man will be at his club.' "

Hartmann kept the appointment. The actress had dismissed the servants and prepared the dinner herself. "After the meal," Sadakichi continued, "she served coffee in the living room. We sat on a huge divan. On the wall above it hung a large painting. I identified its heavy gilt frame as one from the Sears Gallery in Boston. In this frame was a portrait of Sadie's aged lover. It was the most vile piece of work I had seen, and I have seen many, many bad portraits. It was darkly done, crudely brushed, and I couldn't decide whether the stiff face and form in the painting were those of a financier or of a brewery horse in dress clothes. The eyes stared out of a pudding of a face. The picture offended me, and I was glad when our backs were turned to it."

He had an impulse to declare his passion to Sadie, but just as he got down on his knees to make a formal statement of his affections he chanced to raise his eyes to find the portrait staring down upon him. Then the picture-wire broke. The large portrait fell and almost knocked him unconscious. Worse still, Sadie was laughing hysterically.

"Four more years passed by," said Sadakichi in narrating the saga of Sadie Malreaux. "Never mind about my wife; or about another and deeper, more tragic circumstance that I may or may not disclose at a later sitting.

"I now was doing comparatively well, giving lectures on perfumes, and had a studio on Sixth Avenue at Twenty-third Street. There was a saloon nearby that I frequented, and there one day in the back room I again met Sadie. I wish I hadn't. I did not immediately recognize the bloated, tightly corseted woman dressed in red. She had spreading hips and too much rouge on her cheeks, and her once-fresh beauty was gone. The luster had faded from her hair, and dyed red wisps struggled out from beneath the brim of a big flouncing hat with a frowzy ostrich plume on it. She looked like a bad copy of a Gainsborough portrait.

" 'What has happened to you?' I asked when I finally recognized her. 'What in the world?'

"She told me she was lost; lost forever to herself and to the world. We had some drinks, and then I took her to my studio, for she had been put out of her room. My wife was not with me—as though that's anybody's business.

"I remembered the night a woman of the streets had given me shelter. Now I was repaying that debt in part. The next morning Sadie left while I was asleep. There was no note, no inkling as to where she had gone. She was still proud."

Not so many years after this episode Hartmann learned that Sadie was at Blackwell's Island (now Welfare Island) in a prison ward for drug addicts. And there she died.

"There was never any intimacy between us," Sadakichi said. "Yet she was the one woman I would crawl to in eternity. In beauty, *esprit,* and wit she had no equal."

He motioned to his secretary that the dictation was over for the day. When she had left Sadakichi said to me, "Something should be done to make this old beautiful carcass function better than it does. King Duncan died without losing so much blood."

Ere sleep we rub from infant eyes,
We are forever what we are.
                    —Sadakichi

In the summer of 1951 I revisited England. Twenty-five years had gone by since I last had been inside the great art galleries of London town. Unlike many other ports of artistic call, the Tate and the National seemed untouched by the marks of war and the erosions of time.

The masterworks that hang upon the exhibition walls have outlasted governments and kings. Here the pilgrim renews his belief in the longevity of art and is persuaded, as though by painted gospels, that in art, as with religious faith, it is meant for man to rise above himself; and then, with good will and serenity of mind, go on to the last appointment.

The Festival of Britain was in progress, and the year of it happened to be the centenary of the death of Turner. There were two halls hung with his watercolors and oils.

I thought of Sadakichi as I came upon the "Burial at Sea,"

the painting that had excited his cry of "Bravo!" He had spoken to me of Turner's skill in the preparation of colors, how he had ground the pigments with his own hands and compounded them in the liquid vehicle, as many masters before him had done during the golden centuries of art.

On a table in the center of one hall there was an oblong glass case in which Turner's work things had been reassembled in the same way that death had found them at his studio: various glass jars of raw material yet to be ground, the dry pigment powder, mortars and pestles, a hedge of brushes, and a trayful of stoppered pouches of interlaced leather, much worn from the squeezing of their contents to the palette.

Just recently I asked Hugo Ballin for his opinion of the color formulas of the old masters as compared to those used in the manufacture of modern paints. Are the present-day colors as fast? As resistant to the vagaries of climate? The ingredients as well balanced against cracking or peeling?

"The modern paints," he replied, "are just as good, and in many respects even better than the old. It is the modern artist who is not as good."

Back in 1940, and for some time thereafter, the war caused a shortage of imported German paints. John Decker happily came upon four tubes of a certain transparent red, the kind he sometimes overlaid with dramatic effect on his still-life studies.

"These beauties cost me sixty dollars." He caressed the small tubes, then placed them in a shallow drawer of a paint cabinet alongside the easel. An unfinished still-life—

three brown eggs, a deep purple eggplant, a red cabbage, and a bunch of celery—rested on the huge easel. The real hens' eggs and the other subjects were grouped on a nearby table.

Barrymore, Sadakichi, and I were hungry, and a bit thirsty too. Phyllis arrived home with some cans of cold beer and a set of unpainted wall shelves. She asked her husband what color the shelves should be painted.

"Oh," he said, "slap some orange shellac on them. Who gives a damn?"

Notwithstanding his occasional domestic flares, there was no mistaking Decker's love for this self-effacing young woman, nor her devotion to him. The men who frequented Bundy Drive had the highest regard for Phyllis, and with sound reason. Never did she complain when John's friends stayed on and on at the studio; or grumble because of the loud early-morning debates, the debris that convivial men strewed around and about, the short-order meals, the cigarette chars on the floor or on the furniture.

Phyllis Decker had no intellectual pretenses, artistic or otherwise, and she had the good sense not to get in the way of her husband's talent. She managed to stay an artist's wife, a most difficult career indeed.

"She could make her fortune," Barrymore once remarked, "were she to undertake the giving of lessons to wives. I wish some of mine had had her for a tutor."

The day Phyllis brought the wall shelves home, and while Decker was dreamily squeezing paint onto the palette blade, Barrymore said to her, "You don't think you can compete with *that*, do you?"

"No," said she. "I wouldn't even try."

Hartmann meanwhile was in the backyard, roaring for food and drink. We joined him outside for a luncheon of barbecued spareribs. After a time the artist went next door to borrow some more charcoal for the barbecue pit, and on his way back visited his refrigerator for a fresh supply of beer. I heard him laughing uproariously in the kitchen and decided to investigate. I found him howling with merriment at the new wall shelves. Phyllis had emptied three of the expensive tubes of German paint to make the shelves red.

"What a holler!" Decker said. "For one thing, it will take a year for this to dry. For another, Phyllis could have got paint at the dime store and done a much better job. Well, there goes three-fourths of sixty dollars! Whatever three-fourths may be."

To foresee what Decker's response would be to any specific personal event would be a challenge to anyone's powers of clairvoyance. For example, he thought it naïve and charming of Phyllis to have wasted valuable paint on the cheap wall shelves, yet that very night became enraged because she had taken two eggs from the group of still-life subjects. She had scrambled the eggs for Sadakichi.

When Decker saw what had happened to his artistic nest he began to scream and dance. "Dammit!" He got an icebag for his head. "You've screwed up everything! I have a mind to go right out this minute and be unfaithful to you."

Sadakichi returned to Banning again in mid-September. A few weeks later he wrote that he was planning to go to

Detroit and after a stop-over with friends in that city continue on to St. Petersburg, Florida, where one of his daughters had a home. A postscript warned me, "Such a pilgrimage will have to be financed by somebody."

"Don't kick down your stall," I replied by the next mail. "Your oats will be provided."

Upon receipt of my check the old man wrote, not to thank me, for that would have been beneath his dignity, but to say, "I am too great to be noticed. I am the man who died while yet alive, after I served fifty years as Mr. Quick among the dead. The size of your check does not make you a philanthropist."

In late October of 1940 Sadakichi wrote from Detroit that he had visited the zoo. He claimed that the bear-pit resembled Decker's studio, so he had renamed the inhabitants "Barrymore, Decker, Tommy Mitchell, Fowler, etc."

In a letter to Phyllis he accused me of doing him a great injustice. He disregarded the fact that train reservations now were difficult to arrange and charged that I had been most niggardly in not having paid for a drawing room instead of a mere lower berth. He also scolded me for not having had someone accompany him on the journey.

Hartmann stayed on at Detroit for some weeks with a long-time friend, Ben Marx.

Marx was a well-to-do meat-packer who had frequently sent hams, smoked pork sausages, and other products of his establishment to Sadakichi's various California homes.

Mr. Marx had first met Sadakichi in 1909 at Elbert Hubbard's Roycroft Inn at the then-famous essayist and pamphleteer's East Aurora, New York, colony. Sadakichi had gone there to relieve his asthma, and also to rest for a time from his activities as King of New York's Bohemia. He had been at the colony for two years, off and on, by the time Marx arrived.

In writing to me of the Elbert Hubbard days, Mr. Marx (a much younger man than Sadakichi) said he had liked Hubbard and the colony, although the "characters" hovered about the "master," dressed like him, windsor ties and all, and behaved in a manner that seemed somewhat naïve. "Merriam Hubbard, daughter of Elbert's first wife, seemed the superior member of the family after Elbert. The two sons by his second wife were friendly but not in the least arty. They looked after the business affairs at the Roycroft Inn. The meals were excellent, as were the rooms, named after painters, composers, and other notables. Beethoven was my favorite room, for which I usually wired in advance."

Hubbard originally had been a soap salesman for Larkin & Company of Buffalo; had married the daughter of his boss and gone to England on his honeymoon, where he became fascinated by William Morris's Kelmscott Press and artcraft industries. After his return home Hubbard decided to duplicate the Morris enterprises in America. He bought a thousand acres at East Aurora, about eighteen miles south of Buffalo, for this project.

"Lacking the esthetic background for such an achievement," Marx continued, "Hubbard enrolled at Cornell University, where he majored in English literature. He then built the Roycroft Inn, raised cattle, pigs, chickens, and enough garden truck to supply the inn."

During Sadakichi's sojourn at East Aurora, Hubbard had two large presses upon which he printed his magazines *The Philistine* and *The Fra*. Among other accomplishments, Fra Elbertus became the best-known book-designer in America. Marx said that Sadakichi designed not a few of these books and sometimes did ghost-writing under the Hubbard signature.

I myself had known Elbert Hubbard briefly when I was a young newspaperman in Denver. He had come to town as a vaudeville headliner. One of my employers, the colorful Harry H. Tammen of the *Denver Post*, was a Hubbard crony; Hubbard had acquainted him with the works of Emerson and given him a secret recipe to prevent baldness.

I had a real affection for Tammen, and we corresponded frequently after I had gone on to New York. In his will he left cash bequests to several of his employees. As he was drawing up this testament—his wife Agnes afterward told me of this—he said, "I am leaving Fowler an indoor baseball made by Elbert Hubbard, and a copy of Emerson's *Essays*."

"No money?" asked Agnes.

"No money," replied my good friend. "He has no idea of money whatsoever, and it would ruin his career to find out about it too soon."

At the time I met Hubbard, say, in 1912 or 1913, I thought him a bit on the sham side of the fence; a bright but self-centered poseur, a poor-man's Benjamin Franklin. Besides, his *Message to Garcia* had all but wrecked my maiden efforts as a cub reporter.

Having read and absorbed the Hubbard story of Lieu-

tenant Rowan's brave quest, his defiance of the fever-
ridden jungles of Cuba, I observed that he never asked
questions as to how, why, or where he could find Garcia to
deliver the historic message. I made up my mind to emulate
this self-reliant hero. It did not occur to me that the gallant
but close-mouthed lieutenant might have asked the nearest
Associated Press representative where patriot Garcia last
was seen, and thus have spared himself needless delay and
hardship.

When the able but crabby editor of the *Denver Republican,* Josiah M. Ward, assigned me to cover a murder story,
I remembered Lieutenant Rowan's wordless technique. I
went on my mission full of manly confidence, and without
so much as asking Mr. Ward a single question as to the facts
already at hand.

With Elbert Hubbard's fanfare of inspiring prose still
trumpeting in my soul, I did not make inquiries of detec-
tives at the scene of the crime but drew my own conclu-
sions, both as to the motive and the method of the vanished
slayer. The next morning I looked at the front page of the
opposition newspaper to discover that I had been scooped
outrageously. This is the most agonizing experience in the
profession of journalism, and is said to be as painful as a
high-forceps delivery.

From that time on I asked questions of everyone everywhere I went, and regarded Elbert Hubbard as a national
menace.

Ben Marx's letters caused me belatedly to modify my
worst opinions of the long-dead Fra Elbertus. I still thought
he had been quite capable of literary chicaneries, and a

professional soldier in just anyone's advertising legion; but I changed my mind about his personal, human side.

"Contrary to a great many opinions," Marx wrote me, "Hubbard cared little about money. The vaudeville trip was really undertaken to refurbish his bank account. He never sued anybody and always paid any financial claim against him without going to court. One of his secretaries visited the Ford Motor Company, to enter an order for ten thousand copies of *Little Journeys* about Ford and his plant. Henry Ford maintained that he never had ordered these articles and refused to pay for them. Hubbard didn't press the point; nor did he fire the secretary."

Hubbard never drank, never smoked, never wore a hat, and never used eyeglasses; wore his hair long and sported a flowing black tie like Lord Byron's. It somehow sticks in my mind that he had on a floppy black hat when I interviewed him some forty years ago.

"I saw him for the last time," wrote Ben Marx, "on the morning he and Mrs. Hubbard left the inn for their ill-fated voyage on the *Lusitania*."

The outspoken Sadakichi expressed a less generous regard for Hubbard than did Marx. "Fra Elbertus," Hartmann said, "had a slight tinge of craftsmanship in his earlier products; his books, although tawdry-looking at best, attracted popular attention. This active fellow lacked expert knowledge and experience in everything he tried. Communistic principles never entered into his undertakings, but cheap labor did. Mediocre talents cannot produce artistic goods of a high order. His community ended with the running of a scab shop under the pretense of fostering a colony of thinkers and doers. All his employees ever received—I among the others—were token salaries and the privilege of breathing a certain thin intellectual atmosphere that pervaded the holy precincts of the Roycroft shop. There was nothing safe from Hubbard's literary grasp, nothing sacred, either among the living authors or the dead; his wisdom was gathered from every writer who had been translated into English. He did not hesitate to purloin whole pages; he rarely quoted, and, if so, in a most misleading way. His co-workers, including myself, rewrote, suggested, or edited many of his essays. Everyone worked hard; Hubbard also worked prodigiously, but took all the glory. His literary conscience had a weak pulse beat; his writings show no trace of any system, theory, or philosophy. Yet he was a person of great magnetism, of restless energy, clever, and alert. It was impossible to down him, but intellectual somersaults seemed to be his particular gift; and he was like a two-headed monster, with each of the heads smiling, one at the other. He fascinated but did not convince."

It was not until February of 1953 that I learned from the affable Ben Marx how Sadakichi had fared in Detroit, where he had stayed with Marx and other friends in the autumn of 1940. "Clocklike each morning," Marx wrote me, "he would appear at my plant to recline in a large chair he dearly loved. As he watched the meat-cutters he would ask the most astonishing questions concerning the biology of cattle. My men got to like him, and I think he liked them.

"He had expected to stay at our flat, and my wife said all right but that he would have to wait until a visiting cousin left town. Mrs. Marx never was impressed by Hartmann, especially by his views on music, her particular forte. While waiting for the cousin to leave I got quarters for Sadakichi at a hotel, which he didn't like at all. I asked Mrs. Fisher, who conducted an art school, to take him in for a week. She said she would be quite honored to do so."

Mrs. Fisher introduced Sadakichi to her art class. "He passed from easel to easel," Marx wrote, "sneering at each drawing. One admirable thing about Sadakichi was his critical integrity; while in his human relationships he proved impossible to many people. But no unmerited approval was forthcoming from him in matters of art."

At the Fisher house Sadakichi's pipe fumes left a lasting odor among the window drapes. After the fourth day Mrs. Fisher confided to Marx that her guest also was not housebroken and would Marx kindly take over.

"When Sadakichi left our city for the last time," Ben Marx wrote me, "about thirty friends gathered at the train to say farewell. After Hartmann had gone, Russell Legge, an artist for the *Detroit Free Press*, and I had something to drink at the Sheik Café. Legge confessed he had always had a feeling of resentment toward Sadakichi, but added that he admired him for his worldly knowledge, particularly in matters of art."

"Ben, if you died suddenly," said Legge, "Hartmann wouldn't even bother to write."

"That's probably true," Marx replied, "but his restraint would merely be a morbid rejection of polite social form. Let's try him out."

Marx sent Sadakichi a telegram purportedly signed by

his auditor: "Ben died suddenly this morning. Thought you would want to know."

Sadakichi wrote to the supposed widow, saying among other things, "In the presence of death, I am speechless."

Ben Marx mailed a note of apology, an action that enraged Hartmann—but not to a degree that would cause him to forfeit future shipments of meat by his Detroit friend.

While on his way from Detroit to St. Petersburg, Sadakichi was severely bruised in a railway accident. Word of this mishap reached us in his letter of November 27, 1940. On the cold night of November 18, near Akron, Ohio, there had been a thunderous careening of Pullman cars, the breaking of glass, then a blackout of the aisle lamps. The passengers had been in their berths when an ammunition train sideswiped the express, derailed the locomotive, and unbuckled it from the rest of the train.

"I do not exactly know how I got to my daughter's home," his letter continued. "Cuts, scars, bruises. Like Lazarus I have seen death; but never before have I seen the futility of human existence so clearly. . . . Send fifty dollars, and I'll come back to my shack in Banning."

There was a postscript: "Do you still love and admire me? I wonder?"

"This sudden evidence of affection," Barrymore said, "is earth-shaking. Are you quite sure you didn't write it yourself and forge Hartmann's signature?"

In his will Hartmann stipulated, "I leave my periodic shipments of meat to Gene Fowler, to be sent irregularly in moments of whimsy."

TWELVE

Sunshine we want, but also shadows.
Each joy demands its note of pain.
Each cheek must know the fall of tears
That many dream-swept hopes are vain.
                                    —Sadakichi

The day before Christmas, Decker served Tom and Jerry to one and all at his studio. He made the batter with eggs gathered from his own hencoop, and as he laced the substance with liquor remarked that his hens had helped him paint Feodor Ivanovitch Chaliapin as King Lear, a portrait that glared at us from the big easel.

"Some of my Rhode Island Reds," he explained, "escaped from their coop and roosted on a primed board I'd put in the garage to dry. I've painted right over the droppings—and damned if it doesn't heighten the effect."

Someone—Norman Kerry, I think it was—spoke of the Christmas season as a most lonely time for actors when on the road. They felt left out of things, he said, while the towners listened to jingle bells and had someone to whom they could come home drunk.

Barrymore agreed, but said that traveling actors were not

the only victims of melancholia at this time. "I once had a monkey that hated Christmas almost as much as W. C. Fields does. The tree ornaments confused her. She drank herself to death."

This mention of Fields prompted Decker to suggest that we take some Tom and Jerry batter to Uncle Claude's. "If we hurry," he said, "we can reach his place before the sun begins to set."

After Norman Kerry had recited a poetical attack upon the French Foreign Legion—in the ranks of which he had served long ago while trying to forget an emotional injustice—Barrymore, Decker, and I set out by car to pay Uncle Claude a visit.

Upon our arrival Decker manipulated the door-knocker, a device made in the form of a woodpecker. The beak attacked a door panel when a cord was pulled. The electric chimes, like so many other things at W. C.'s house, had long been out of kilter.

There was a loudspeaker above the door, by means of which Uncle Claude would respond from his upstairs hideaway to the pecking of the wooden bird—sometimes with startling effect. The cunning old chap had a good view of the grounds and of the path of entrance to his house, a long, cloisterlike approach shielded by a pergola over which vines of wild grape struggled to keep alive. When the comedian saw friends approaching he would wait until they used the woodpecker and then call out various insults, some of them quite bawdy, or utter words of endearment in falsetto voice.

One time while I was visiting with Fields, two nuns, probably seeking a subscription to some worthy charity,

were spied by him as they walked along the pathway toward the house. Before they even had a chance to knock
W. C. set up such a din over the loudspeaker that the good
sisters revised their plans.

Fields simulated the violent quarrel of lovers—snarled in
his own voice, then answered himself in falsetto. There were
threats by the male voice, piteous entreaties by the artificial
voice, such as, "I'll murder you with this baseball bat, you
double-crossing tart!" "Don't! Please don't beat me again,
Murgatroyd! Think of poor little Chauncey, our idiot child!"

"Bill," I scolded, "you have no right to do such a thing
to those good sisters."

With the big binoculars fixed to his eyes he stood at the
east window like an admiral on the bridge of a flagship. "I
don't want just anyone that I don't know coming here," he
said, scanning the horizon of his private world. "And I don't
even want many people I *do* know."

That late afternoon before Christmas there was no response at first to the knocking of the wooden bird. Decker
again pulled the cord.

The voice of Gregory LaCava sounded over the loudspeaker. "Who is it?"

"Peer Gynt and his mother," said Barrymore.

"Oh! That you, Jack?"

"I'm not quite sure."

"Bill's not feeling too hot. I'll be right down."

It seemed there had been another servants' strike, so we
waited for LaCava to let us in. He preceded us upstairs.
"Bill had quite an experience a little while ago," he said on
the way. "He's kind of upset."

Uncle Claude was a good sixty-three years old—or a bad sixty-three, depending upon one's viewpoint—and though he refused to quit work, saying that a retired man was bound to rest himself into the grave—he occasionally admitted that he was "living on velvet from here on in."

In the office our friend was leaning against the bar, his broad back to us. He was immaculately dressed, as though he had just returned from a formal call. In a trembling hand he held a triple martini. On the wall behind the bar hung a photograph of Fields and Miss Mae West, in which he was pictured tugging at the corset strings of the bosomy actress. It was a scene from a screenplay in which each star had stopped just this side of manslaughter in trying to outdo the other. Fields was staring at this photograph, and at first we assumed that Miss West at last had found a way to deflate our pal; sent him a poisoned watermelon or a lock of a film-producer's hair.

"Bad omen!" he was saying through his teeth. "Bad omen!"

"What's the matter, Billy?" Decker asked with much concern.

"It was the damnedest thing!" LaCava said. "Will you have a beer? Or a drop of the creature?"

"What's it all about?" I inquired of W. C. "Are you ill?"

Fields faced us and said with a show of good manners, "Make yourselves at home." Then he turned again to gaze at the photograph of Miss West. "Drat!" He sucked at his martini. "Drat!"

"It was this way," said LaCava as Decker handed him the pasteboard container of Tom and Jerry batter. "Some dame who lived up the road wanted for a long time to meet Bill. Wrote him daily fan letters, telegrams, tried to get him on the telephone, even sent flowers to the house."

Fields left the bar and crossed the room to his big desk. "Wouldn't take no for an answer," he complained. "Day after day. It was gruesome."

"Well, this old bastard here," said LaCava, "is guilty of everything; suspects everybody, even us; and always turned her down. But she kept it up and up; and today, while we were sitting here, knocking everybody except Gene Buck, this lady's Filipino butler came over and—"

Fields interrupted with a snarl, "It was all your fault! You dago lettucehead! Why did you let him in here in the first place?"

LaCava, as Fields' intimate friend, was used to his insults. "All right. I'll admit I did let this Filipino in. How was I to know he wanted to sell you a bill of goods?"

"I must have softening of the brain!" Our host glared at us as though awaiting confirmation of the self-diagnosis. "The last thing I want these days is to meet a dame."

"Well, anyway," LaCava continued, "the Filipino boy said it was his madam's dearest wish to see her hero. This broken-down juggler is a ham at heart, and the flattery got through to him finally. He dressed, as you can see, in his heartbreaker's outfit, while I mixed martinis in the rubber keg; and then we took it with us up the hill to call on this lady."

"It was fantastic!" said Uncle Claude. "Jack, *you* should have been there. Lionel too."

"Why don't we go now?" inquired Jack. "Is she young?"

"Wait," LaCava said. "I thought something was peculiar about the whole place. Awful quiet, and the smell of flowers. The Filipino bowed us into the parlor, and there—good Lord! There was a coffin, open, and a dead dame in it!"

"He ain't kidding," said Fields. "Stretched out cold!"

"And while we stood there gawking," said LaCava, "the Filipino boy came over to the casket and addressed the dead woman. 'He's here, madam. Mr. Fields is here. And you have met him now, like you always wanted.' And then the Filipino turned to Bill and said, 'Mr. Fields, this is my madam. Meet my madam. Madam, meet Mr. Fields.'"

There was a moment of silence before the irreverent Decker asked, "Did she acknowledge the introduction?"

"Go to hell, will you?" shouted Uncle Claude. "I just don't like dead people!"

"You don't even like live ones," LaCava said.

Fields' experience had put him in a mood so black that not even a mug of Decker's Tom and Jerry cheered him. "Why do these things happen to me?" moaned Fields, as if putting the question to the world at large. "Fate simply hates my guts!"

After our visit Decker dropped me off at my home. Toward midnight I received word that he was in jail. It seems that by the time he and Barrymore returned to the studio the Christmas Eve guests had drunk up all the liquor. Decker went out in his car to replenish his stock. After calling upon friends here and there, he managed to collect ten or twelve bottles.

While Decker was driving home, two policemen in a prowl car signaled for him to pull over to the curb. They came upon the several bottles and decided to take Decker in for a sobriety test. The doctor at the police station happened to be a man of extremely short stature.

"What do you do for a living?" he asked Decker.

"I'm a portrait painter."

"Do you think," said the little doctor, looking up at Decker, "that you would be able to paint a portrait of me in your present conditions?"

"No," Decker replied, "I don't paint miniatures."

This remark cost the artist's friends three hundred dollars.

THIRTEEN

*I make a bed of sun and sand
Beside some vanished stream.*
—Sadakichi

The house I lived in was a big one, and it had a big yard with beautiful trees and shrubs, and in that yard a black great Dane named Lily did as she pleased.

Lily, when full-grown, weighed one hundred and thirty pounds but insisted upon being a lapdog, a whim that compelled me to lean out to either side of her sleek black barrel of a body if I wished to see or converse with a guest seated opposite me. Lenient though I was with all my pets, I would not permit Lily to sit on my lap when I was writing a story—although some of my work might indicate that she not only sat there but guided the quill. Another of Lily's habits was to thrust her forepaws against a victim and send him sprawling among the hedges. It was like being straight-armed, double-strength, by a Notre Dame fullback. In self-defense I taught Lily to run between my straddling legs, to be held there in a body-scissors while I petted her.

If an unwary caller chanced to spread his feet apart, Lily would instantly make use of this wicket. Just such a thing occurred one dark night after my young friend Charles Lederer had had a slight misunderstanding with one of my guests and decided to take leave of the house. On his way out Charles mistook the back door for the front. Outside, he paused momentarily on the lawn for some dead-reckoning, and the unseen Lily dashed between his legs, then galloped off with the confused gentleman jockey on her back.

Although Lederer was a young man of extraordinary courage I could not help observing his pallor when he returned inside. He seemed temporarily chastened as he sipped a restorative and forgave everyone's trespasses. Perhaps the Hound of Heaven had caught up with him.

Lily disliked but one member of my household, Chester the parrot. (I regarded Chester as a male because he was so self-centered.) Lily used to stare at my green and yellow friend as he did slow acrobatic exercises among the branches of a tree. During this bird-watching the jealous Lily conducted herself with admirable restraint. Any lady, in these circumstances, is supposed to act in an aloof manner toward a known rival. However, I felt that Hollywood had corrupted Lily's good manners; and if so, she would be satisfied with nothing less than a bloodbath and the dismemberment of her foe.

There was a strong suggestion made by Mrs. Hubbard, my mother-in-law (who had been bitten now and again by Chester), that the parrot be given to a Mr. Harper, whose young daughter wanted this bird more than anything else.

I hesitated to part with Chester, even though I felt that Lily would one day close her jaws upon him.

Chester and I had been pals for fifteen years. He had become so fond of me that he would permit me, after a brisk round of infighting, to manicure his nails. Moreover, I liked Chester's singing voice. He preferred the classics, and one of the best numbers in his repertoire was the opening phrase of Tosti's "Good-by." Chester would sing this on cue, sincerely, and in a fine whisky tenor, like that of W. C. Fields. I would prompt Chester to croon this farewell whenever a guest had begun to wear out his welcome.

John Barrymore was fond of both Lily and Chester. As I have written elsewhere, he had an amazing way of winning the trust of birds and animals, however wild or shy.

One rainy morning in January of 1941, shortly after daybreak, I heard loud voices and repeated hammerings at my front door. It sounded like the siege of Constantinople. It was Barrymore and Decker.

I got out of bed and went to the head of the stairs. The butler, sleepy-eyed and in his dressing gown, already had opened the hall door. Barrymore announced that he was the Patriarch of Jerusalem, but my man knew him all too well and told him that he and his companion (who said he was the Emperor Diocletian, traveling incognito) were unwelcome at this or any other hour.

The butler was a wonderful fellow, firm of muscle and of mind, an ex-wrestler. He was of the unshakable opinion that my mother-in-law was the head of the house—as, come to think of it, she may have been. She had told him that certain of my cronies, Barrymore and Decker in particular, were evil influences upon her hard-working son-in-law and were, under all circumstances, to be denied the house.

Mrs. Hubbard was wholly unimpressed by men of talent, let alone men of genius. She had seen many of them come and go—frequently to hell, as she expressed it. During her girlhood in Missouri she oftentimes had listened to Mark Twain telling his stories to the children of the town. When I learned of this I at once asked Mrs. Hubbard to repeat some of the great man's sayings.

"Let me think," she said. "You mean old Sam Clemens? Yes, I saw him almost every day."

"Tell me everything that you remember—what he did, what he said, how he looked."

"Well"—she seemed anxious to dismiss the whole thing—"he smelled of whisky and tobacco, but he did have nice hair."

If Mark Twain had failed to impress her, how could one expect her to admire Barrymore, W. C. Fields, Thomas Mitchell, Gregory LaCava, or Decker? As for Sadakichi Hartmann, the things he could do and did to a bathroom floor put him a thousand light-years outside the pale.

When, this rainy January dawn, I heard the ex-wrestler tell Barrymore and Decker to go away, I hastily returned to my bedroom and crossed over to a French window, the doors of which opened on an outside balcony. The rain was making machine-gun sounds on the balcony awning; a wind was blowing in from the sea; but I managed to advise the Patriarch and the Emperor to enter through an un-latched garden gate.

"I'll meet you in the breakfast room," I called down. "Give me time for a shower."

"We're having one now," Decker shouted. "What we need is a stiff drink."

I appeared in the breakfast room some fifteen or twenty minutes later. Barrymore was sitting crouched forward in front of the parrot's cage, repeating with careful inflection, again and again, just two words, one of which I cannot set down with propriety. Of course, were I to write a praise-worthy novel, it would be my artistic duty to use this and kindred bits of realism on every page. I shall but venture to say that the latter word of the Barrymore slogan was the commonly acceptable "you," with a short Anglo-Saxon verb of provocative biological import galvanizing the personal pronoun.

"Good morning, gentlemen," I said. "Why didn't you wear raincoats?"

"No interruptions if you please," Barrymore admonished me. "I'm giving Chester an elocution lesson."

As the man of superb diction returned to his task I observed that the bird was perched low, its yellow head cocked to one side, obviously trying to master the words.

"Chester is an excellent study," Decker said. "What about that drink?"

With Barrymore still rehearsing the parrot I went to the pantry for refreshments, delivered them, then decided to dress for the day. Later on, as we left my house to go to Bundy Drive, I said good-by as usual to Chester. He paid no attention to me and continued to mutter to himself. He seemed in an introspective mood.

At Decker's studio we were pleasantly surprised to find the long-absent Sadakichi Hartmann seated at the dining-room table, eating some strange-looking concoction.

"Oho!" said Barrymore. "The lean and hungry-looking Cassius is with us once again."

Our hero-elect merely waved a fork; otherwise he ignored our greetings. Phyllis Decker had let him in, but for once had been too sleepy to make breakfast. Hartmann had gone to the refrigerator to help himself and by some mistake had selected, it turned out, a plate of horsemeat prepared for Decker's dogs.

That evening, after my day's work at Culver City, I dropped by at Decker's. Hartmann informed me that he had decided at last to set down the story of his extramarital experience with a New England poetess. He showed me some ten pages typed by the secretary and several letters the poetess had written, which he had kept all these years.

Sadakichi had selected ten of her many letters with a view to publishing them posthumously under the title "Letters to a Married Man." His intention, he said, was to edit this correspondence and write a foreword under the pseudonym "Sidney Allan." He had answered but two or three of these poignant letters, and, indeed, seemed to have behaved unchivalrously toward her in several other respects.

It was in May 1899 that Sadakichi met the young New England poetess, whom we shall call Martha, for convenience' sake. He was still married to Betty, and by now had two sons and three daughters by her. The poetess was unmarried.

"She had a New England conscience," he said, "which was constantly at war with her fierce desire to be an active force in the women's emancipation movement. She wanted to have a child by a literary man without marriage; but after she had it, wanted the man too. She had such widespread connections all over the New England states that the illegitimate birth caused an awful scandal, and for years I was barred from lecturing in New England. Her letters were a chronicle of the emotions of a high-minded New England woman, an authoress, who, influenced even against her own convictions by the liberal preachments of the all-out feminists of the day, chose to burden her life with the problem of motherhood outside wedlock. The impress upon her supersensitive mind was great when New England wrath fell upon her. The recurrent self-accusation and doubt over the moral validity of her action returned over and over again to that one cry of pain: 'It was wrong!' The struggle to justify it to herself, and then the unconquerable attachment to her lover and the father of her child, these things formed a commentary on the problems of women's emancipation—as it would in some circles even now."

In Martha's first letter, in June 1900, soon after her illegitimate son Robert was born, she expressed the hope that Sadakichi would come to see their child. In a subsequent letter she said she had returned briefly to her native New England, notwithstanding the scorn of her fellows, and, with her child, was residing for the time being in a room afforded by one of her braver cousins. Life in her native community became difficult for Martha, what with the meager allowance afforded her by her outraged parents, and the scornful attitude of the neighbors. She left New England for an out-of-the-way place in New Jersey. There she lived on top of a mountain, she wrote, but only in the physical sense, not the spiritual.

The correspondence shows her to have been a gentlewoman of superior mind; neurotic perhaps, but forthright and brave. She discussed in a lively fashion the new books she managed to come by, pictures she saw or remembered, as well as certain musical compositions with which she seemed quite familiar. She spoke of Sadakichi's writing a symphony—a side of his genius that no one else seemed aware of, then or thereafter. (It was a way of his, when not boasting of what he already had accomplished, to talk profusely about some mighty project he planned to undertake. Perhaps a symphony was one of the many facets of his wishful-thinking process.)

For several years she wandered from place to place, but for the most part her letters showed no bitterness. There were womanly pleas, to be sure, that Sadakichi come to this or that hideaway. She tried to appear patient, even lighthearted, but at times let her guard down to admit that the poetic fire burned low and that a feeling of despair came over her each night, preventing sleep. Martha told of a game she played to quiet the demon of loneliness. She would write a long letter to Sadakichi, keep it for a day or two, reread it, and pretend that it really was a love letter written by him instead of one written by her to Hartmann.

Occasionally she gave way to growing despair, saying that "a great many things are in ashes for good and all." Then, as if to reprove herself for whimpering, she would say in the very next sentence that there was nothing to do but go on, the burned-out fires behind; and that one could even smile and look back to find many things about which one might become tranquil in the remembrance—"things which we ourselves wish either were beginning anew, or buried for all time."

In one letter Martha declared that she no longer cared what people surmised or said of her; but merely hoped to keep them from annoying her "actively." When former friends chanced to come upon her at some temporary haven, or while she was seeking employment, the sadistic busy-bodies would proceed at once to disclose her identity.

As the years passed she made several plans for a reunion with the father of her child. In one instance she suggested that he visit her in New Jersey and pose as her cousin. But nothing came of this or of her other bids for happiness. She could but keep on swimming upstream in the fast-flowing river of make-believe.

Whenever she changed her residence—and she found it necessary to do so quite frequently—she was plagued by such personal questions as, why didn't she, a young widow, wear black? There were many embarrassing inquiries whenever she applied for, or briefly held, a clerical job. She finally decided to change her name to Miss So-and-So, offering in explanation that she was a disciple of the emancipated Miss Lucy Stone and, as such, pledged to guard her status as an individualist. This unorthodox stand only worsened her plight in a generation not yet used to the ways of purposeful women.

Once Martha wrote that she again had paid a visit to

her relatives. She described their "about-face," their advice
to "wear the scarlet letter openly," confess her wrongdoing,
and remain at her parents' home to prosper as best she
might. She refused to do this, saying that she would be
constantly subjected to accusations, as well as "mere tol-
eration" on the part of her female cousins and aunts. She
said she had never intended to solve a sex problem; nor, on
the other hand, to pose as a martyr in the cause of unmarried motherhood. However, for her to enter upon a lifelong
public repentance for something she herself regarded as an
expression of womanly independence would be to confess to
her little world a guilt she would not admit even to herself.
It would make of her a Hester Prynne. Her one regret was
that her action had not been quite just to the child.

For a time her courage and her pride left her. She cried
out, not so much against the man himself as against the con-
ventional world. She was writing to him, she said, with a
blanket draped about her shoulders, for it was cold, and she
felt "weary, maimed, and broken."

For almost four years these letters went out to the man
who so seldom answered them. She knew he had received
her letters, for none had been returned to her. Martha told
Sadakichi that her ambition now was not to be a great poet,
or even a good one, but to have the right to enjoy humble
domestic duties and womanly relations, and to know that
"greatest of treasures, a perfect home, with no feverish looking backward at youth."

Toward the close of this one-way correspondence Martha
—quite unreasonably, to Sadakichi's way of thinking—wrote
a letter of renunciation. In it she revealed the torments

she had for so long a time endured. It was not so much, she said, that her heart had been hurt, or that her youth, her life even, had been cut off from every future possibility of love and happiness, as it was the strong inference she must draw from his cold silence to her questions; the probability that he thought she had been wrong in having loved him, and he in having loved her. That, she said, was the cruelest bitterness, beyond which there was no relief but death.

Even as she wrote this letter, however, she absolved him of all personal blame and preferred to think him sincere and high-minded. She did not wish to believe that he cared only to destroy. Although he had been a full partner in the wrong-doing, she could survive if he would assure her now that he had not then seen other than good in their passion. However, if she was willing to bear her side of the trouble, as well as the grief that came of it, he should at least *help* her to bear it, and help her withstand the hardship of it; at the very least send her a word of friendly understanding.

She pointed out that she had never been "one of those imbecile women who have worshiped you, rushing about after you, because they live in a morbid state of excitement all the time."

Toward the conclusion of this long letter the writer abruptly departed from her years of effort to spare him blame. It was as though a flimsy bridge quite suddenly had given way beneath her feet and plunged her into the depths. Never before, she said, had she cursed anyone. But now, having lived through a terrible trial, it was more than human nature could bear. He must know that she had never been content with the inferior loves that many times had been offered her. Instead, she had waited for a love that she could feel in her heart was a real love. She had thought theirs was that great love, for her soul, she said, had adored him.

"But I now know it never could have been love at all—because love is fire and iron. And it was wicked to give me anything that was not good and true. It was all wrong then, and the world may so well end for me. My nature is shaken to its depths, and my life is a horrible disaster."

In the next mail Martha posted a letter of denunciation in which she referred to Sadakichi as "the trashy philanderer with the hangdog look of a knave when caught"; and as "one who hovers about a cheap bohemia, and who imagines that a short-lived picturesqueness, which finally turns to unattractiveness, deceives any but children or fools for long."

Many years passed before Sadakichi again heard from Martha. She wrote from Italy that Robert had grown up to be a strong though gentle person, had enlisted in the army and gone to France in 1918. She too had gone abroad, with the Red Cross.

Robert and his mother met overseas when he was on leave in Paris. He brought her some white asters, she said, his favorite flowers. After this short respite Robert rejoined his outfit at the battlefront and his mother resumed her duties as a Red-Cross worker.

Robert subsequently wrote his mother that he was about to be given another short leave, and could she meet him in Paris. She prepared a room for him at a pension and put a vase of white asters on a table beside his bed.

"He never came to look at the white new flowers," the

last letter from Martha to Sadakichi said, "and so perished my dearest hope—under the poppies of Flanders."

The strange man that was Sadakichi Hartmann said to me at Decker's studio, "After Robert's death the meaning of life became obscure to me. I lost interest in the pattern of it."

The morning after I heard the story of Martha and read her letters to a married man I came downstairs for a late breakfast. The story had made me sad, and even the presence of Gregory LaCava at the table did not at once cheer me.

Greg had stopped over at my house on his way to see Uncle Claude. He was going to try to persuade Fields not to sue a minor comedian for stealing one of his routines and using it in some clap-trap nightclub on Western Avenue.

"In the first place," said LaCava, "Fields stole this routine himself thirty years ago."

"You know," I said as I looked about the familiar breakfast room, "something is missing." Chester was gone, cage and all.

When my ex-wrestler servant came in with the bacon and eggs I asked, "Where's Chester?"

"He's gone."

"Gone where?"

"Does Mr. LaCava wish orange juice?" he asked. He seemed evasive.

"To the devil with Mr. LaCava! Where's Chester?"

He replied with great dignity, "Chester insulted Mrs. Hubbard."

"Now come on," I said. "Tell me the plain facts."

"Mrs. Hubbard telephoned Mr. Harper early this morning, sir. He just left with Chester."

LaCava had an inkling of some domestic crisis, and mentioned that he had seen someone drive off with a parrot just as he got out of his own car.

"Nobody consulted me," I said. "That is, not lately. I'll see about this." Then an idea occurred to me. "*How* did Chester insult my mother-in-law?"

The ex-wrestler hesitated. "It happened when Mrs. Hubbard said 'Good morning, Chester,' like she always does."

"Then what?"

"I would prefer not to say."

"But I insist. Did Chester say anything?"

"If you please. It was all very shocking."

"What did Chester say?"

"When Mrs. Hubbard said her 'Good morning, Chester,' he said the bad words Mr. Barrymore was teaching him only yesterday."

When LaCava learned the facts of the elocution lesson he almost fell out of his chair with laughter. I reluctantly decided that it was best to let Chester go; for he had found —or rather talked his way into—a wonderful home, where no jealous animals sought to harm him.

I can still hear Greg LaCava saying, "I hope that Chester is watching his language."

FOURTEEN

In this torn sea of arabesques,
Looms there no isle of peace?
　　　　—Sadakichi

Everyone should know better than to ask a celebrated actor "How do you feel today?" Any inquiry as to his health, or the lack of it, quite likely will be construed as a sign that he is only mortal and already has one buskin in the grave.

With three of my most talented friends—John Barrymore, W. C. Fields, and John Decker—taking turns at falling ill in 1941, I frequently put aside my good manners to ask them how they were feeling. Not that I received satisfactory answers from men who walked where not only angels, but devils, feared to tread.

Barrymore usually would reply, "Never felt better in my life." He would say this even when at the hospital, and would protest that he had been brought there against his will. It was his habit to escape, as soon as the nurse's back was turned, and proceed to relight what little there was left of the candle, at both ends.

In like manner, though more belligerently of course, W. C. Fields sought to avoid discussion of his various illnesses. Now and again he might concede that he felt low in the mind and that evil influences were at work against him. On one occasion (the time he learned he had become a grandparent) he said, "How do I feel? I feel as sad as a streetwalker's father."

Decker was almost as reluctant as the others to discuss matters touching upon his health. If he placed an icebag on his head we knew neuralgia had crowned him. One day he blurted out that he was going to hang himself from one of the brown crossbeams of his studio. Obviously he was in great pain at the time; but instead of committing suicide he began to paint one of his best portraits, "The Royal Vagabond." This much-admired work pictured John Barrymore wearing clown's rags, with a miniature high hat cocked on his head, and in his hand a scepter that had for its top a cabbage as a mock-symbol of sovereignty.

In speaking to me of our mutual friend Barrymore, the late dean of drama critics Ashton Stevens said, "Nobody can run downhill as fast as a thoroughbred." His remark applied as well to Fields and Decker. My three friends were severally up and down like groggy but gallant pugilists in the spring of 1941. Decker collapsed one day at his easel from a gastric hemorrhage. He was given blood transfusions at the Cedars of Lebanon Hospital. When W. C. Fields visited him, Decker roused and managed to sketch his visitor and himself receiving alcohol drips in their arm veins from a two-way bottle of rum.

"The doctors claim I have diabetes," Decker told W. C. "I must weigh every ounce of food, take insulin, and not even read the label on a brandy bottle."

"Pay no attention to those dastardly fee-splitters," said W. C. Fields, himself doggedly resisting the inroads on his liver and kidneys. "When doctors and undertakers meet they always wink at each other."

Uncle Claude's dislike of medical men—not excepting Hippocrates and the Mayos—had been strengthened, if possible, by one of his recent experiences at court, when he had spent several days in litigation at Riverside while resisting payment of a doctor's fee of several thousand dollars. He had not been satisfied merely to sit in the hall of justice on hot summer days and cool himself with a fan, upon which could be seen the picture of an almost naked bathing beauty. He had demanded that martinis be served at the counsel table.

The civil suit was tried without a jury, because, Fields had said, "It is impossible to find twelve fair men in all the world. Perhaps we can have better luck with only one, the judge."

Fields' lawyer persuaded the court that his client had to be given tonic doses of alcohol, else the arteries might spring a leak. In granting this unusual privilege His Honor decreed that no bottles or telltale glasses be displayed while court was in session. At his hotel Fields filled his red rubber keg to the gunwales, then brought it to court, and every half-

hour or so would pour a martini into a paper cup. Between
sips W. C. would beam upon His Honor, then leer at any
witness who dared testify against him, whispering to his
counsel such words as "Judas!" or "Benedict Arnold!" or
"Lying son-of-a-bitch!"

The judge behaved so courteously that Uncle Claude believed he had the bench solidly on his side. Sometimes the
comedian would discreetly raise his Lily cup a few inches,
as though to drink the jurist's good health.

Imagine W. C.'s rage when, after the evidence on both
sides had been submitted, the bench promptly, and perhaps enthusiastically, ruled in favor of the plaintiff. The de-
feated comedian risked contempt of court to cry out,
"Rooked! Rooked! I've been had!"

On his way back to Los Angeles, Fields said to his chauffeur, "Why didn't someone tell me this judge was a tee-
totaler? We are living on a hostile planet. Next time I'll get
a change of venue to the jurisdiction of some trustworthy
sot."

W. C. stayed incommunicado at his home for two or three
days after this legal and financial setback. He refused to
report for work at his motion-picture studio, and when an
impatient executive telephoned again and again the comedian instructed his manservant, "Give him an evasive answer."

This man was new at the Fields household, where the
turnover of servitors always was considerable. He had an
exceptionally small head, with a point to it, and perhaps
that was why W. C. had hired him.

When the picture executive telephoned for perhaps the

sixth time Fields shouted, "Didn't I tell you to give him an evasive answer?"

"Yes, sir, but *what* evasive answer am I to give?"

Fields supplied the evasive answer. He ordered his man to tell the picture executive to accomplish upon his own person a most impractical physical deed, a feat that even the world's most agile contortionist would be unable to perform.

While the servant was somewhat gingerly carrying out the instructions W. C. kept squinting at the back of the man's Gothic-style head. "I can't understand why he's content to work as a domestic," Fields said. "With a head like that he should own Hollywood."

Early in 1941 Barrymore entered the hospital with a severe gastric condition; next day he took French leave of the place. I was quite familiar with his social ports of call and soon came upon him at a favorite restaurant. He refused to admit that he was ill, and to substantiate his claim of sound health suggested we call on the convalescing Decker.

We found the artist at work at his easel. He had on a bedraggled smock that could have belonged, in point of age and grime and dried paint smears, to Fra Filippo Lippi the Florentine. Because of his strict diet Decker had lost much weight. The smock hung from his big bones like a maternity gown the day after the blessed event.

"I'm damned," Decker told us, "if I can get the right nuance of blue-green that I want as a background sheen for this picture. God, but I'm hungry!"

Decker was painting a portrait of Errol Flynn from memory, as was his common practice. Although most forgetful in many respects, the artist had a remarkable pictorial memory. He did not like to have his subjects sit for him; instead he would study them at their own homes or at public places, then retire to his studio to do their portraits.

"The women sitters distract me by their chit-chat," he would say, "and the men want a drink; and then we both forget all about the work at hand."

While Decker was endeavoring to come upon the wished-for blue-green we heard a small explosion in the kitchen and then the hissing of steam. Decker hastily put aside his brush and palette and went on the double-quick to the kitchen. Barrymore and I followed.

Instead of paying the least attention to the escaping gas from the drowned-out burner the artist pointed happily to the ceiling. "That's it! Exactly what I'm after. The perfect shade of blue-green!"

I turned off the gas. "What were you boiling?"

"Oh"—he kept right on admiring some bluish-green splotches on the ceiling—"the doctor told me to take a specimen of my urine, as a guide to the insulin shots, and mix it with some stuff he gave me, then boil it for a litmus-paper test. I was so busy painting Flynn that I forgot. As you can see, the kettle blew the lid. What a wonderful blue-green! Perfect for a Flynn background!"

"In similar circumstances," Barrymore observed, "Archimedes would have changed his triumphant cry of 'Eureka!' to 'Urethra!'"

Decker went to get his palette, a brush, and some paint tubes, then climbed onto the stove to have a closer view of the ceiling blotches. Painstakingly he proceeded to match their tonal value on his palette. As we were looking on we heard the barking of Decker's several dogs, and then the wheezing Sadakichi Hartmann came into the house by way of the kitchen door.

He had been ill again in Banning, he said. A doctor-passenger on the bus had asked him to describe his symptoms, and he had replied, "I have symptoms of immortality."

Sadakichi studied the stove-standing artist for a few moments, then asked, "Are you cooking yourself for dinner?"

Hartmann insisted that I notify his secretary that he was on the scene. She was to come at once to Decker's studio to take down his "next to last words." The young woman canceled an appointment at the beauty parlor, arrived at Decker's within the hour, and set to work.

After Sadakichi was divorced from Betty Walsh Hartmann he married a Quaker, Lillian Bonham. He refused to discuss this marriage, beyond stating the fact that he and his second wife went from New York to live in San Mateo, California. There Sadakichi suffered from asthma much of the time, but managed to rewrite several chapters of a work called *Passport to Immortality*. The Hartmanns later moved to Beaumont.

"Like the Emperor Nero," he said, "I have always been misunderstood. Nero wanted to burn down the slums, nothing more; but the wind changed, and all Rome burned. Everywhere I lived I was regarded as a dangerous freak: because I dealt in truth. Truth more often than not is both unwelcome and dangerous."

Ever since 1910, he went on to say, he had been hounded

by secret-service men, policemen, private investigators, and stool pigeons. As an example of this chronic persecution, he recalled a personal incident that occurred soon after the United States entered the First World War. He had gone from Beaumont to San Francisco, upon learning that the saloon-keepers there were prospering enormously because of the patronage of shipyard workers. He took with him a large supply of his pamphlets and books.

"When these war-workers drank," Hartmann said, "and especially when they became drunk, they had another kind of thirst: a desire to improve their minds. They wanted to know what to read. I recommended Chesterfield (not the cigarette of that name) as a means for them to learn better manners, and my own works to give them culture. I sold my pamphlets and books at the bars every day, at very good prices."

Poet George Sterling obtained a part-time job for Sadakichi at the Bohemian Club. One day several Army officers, among them a military surgeon from the Presidio, were having something to drink at the club. They invited Hartmann to join them for a friendly glass or two or three. The surgeon spoke about German atrocities as reported from war-struck towns of Belgium.

Sadakichi remarked, "In time of war *all* soldiers of invading armies commit atrocities."

One of the officers said to Sadakichi, "You surely don't mean *our* boys?"

"*All* soldier boys," replied Hartmann. "American or Roman, French or Greek or—"

The officer interrupted sternly, "I beg your pardon! You

cannot make remarks like that about our boys. May I remind you that seditious talk is a crime?"

"And may I remind you," replied Hartmann, "that you are committing a crime while drinking in uniform?"

Hartmann was bounced from the club, and several days later was arrested at his San Mateo home. The police took him to jail in Redwood City. When Sadakichi inquired as to the nature of the charge against him, his jailer merely told him that he could see and talk to no one.

"Can I depend upon that?" Hartmann said.

When court convened the next morning a bailiff informed Sadakichi that the charge against him was seditious utterance. Hartmann balked at going inside the courthouse, a building he described as "a baroque abortion." He demanded that he be tried outdoors, under a tree that had limbs stout enough to support his weight in the event of hanging.

At the preliminary arraignment the judge said to Sadakichi, "You don't believe in militarism?"

"I never said so in my books," Hartmann replied.

"I haven't read your books," the judge said.

"I can understand that. Hah!"

The judge released Sadakichi without bail, provided he go to work in the shipyards until the day of his trial, entered on the court calendar for two weeks hence.

Hartmann reported at the yards but stayed only an hour or so among the shipwrights. The next day he once again found himself in jail for having violated the terms of his temporary freedom.

"Why did you leave the shipyards?" he was asked.

"I did not like the design of the hulls. These cargo ships

you're building are ugly; and I do not care for that or any other kind of man-made ugliness."

Sterling retained John S. Catlen to defend Hartmann. The lawyer persuaded the trial judge to hear the case in chambers. "Your Honor," he said, "this man is a poet."

"Yes," said the judge, "I have seen some of it. But he writes without rhyme. How can he be a poet? Like Bryant, for example? *Thanatopsis.*"

"Bryant's *Thanatopsis*," Sadakichi said, "has no rhyme."

"That cannot be," the judge replied.

A copy of Bryant's works was procured from the public library. When the judge saw for himself that *Thanatopsis* contained no rhyme he had a more generous regard for the prisoner's intelligence and placed him on probation.

"But," he warned, "you must quit drinking. Otherwise I'll have to give you a stiff sentence."

At a celebration held at Paul Elder's bookstore Hartmann gave a lecture on Joseph Conrad. He got halfway through it —and all the way through a bottle of whisky. A probation officer reported this moral lapse to the judge.

"Let him alone," said the jurist. "I only wish I dared speak my mind as freely as Hartmann does—and still be re-elected to public office."

Sadakichi left his Beaumont home in 1922 to return briefly to New York's Greenwich Village. "It was at about this time," Decker said, "that I met Sadakichi. I was doing the scenic designs for the *Greenwich Village Follies,* and also working as a caricaturist for the theatrical pages of the *Evening World.*"

Sadakichi nodded in agreement. "Modern civilization was

dying then. You could hear the death rattle in the music, a fermented noise; and in art see the linoleum-makers' feeling for design. Literature was faring somewhat better than the other arts, but it too smelled of death, and had for its main theme the story of lost men in a hopeless world."

"There was a would-be sculptress who had a studio in Washington Mews," Decker recalled. "She was one of those wretched beings with one-nineteenth of a talent and lots of alimony. She announced to a select circle that she was going to unveil her latest masterpiece on such-and-such a night. I told Sadakichi about this chance to free-load, and we invited ourselves to the shindig. We found many social blossoms there, as well as the usual coterie of half-assed sycophants and poseurs who think that by rubbing up against bad art they can become good artists."

For an hour or two before the unveiling, Decker continued, the guests swilled booze of bootleg origin. He and Sadakichi surreptitiously went to the upstairs studio to preview the sculptress's latest achievement. That work, hooded with a damp cloth, stood on a pedestal in the center of the room. Sadakichi unswathed the object. It was a large hand done in modeling clay, with the fingers opened halfway, the palm extended upward.

Decker spied some plasticine and was prompted to use this material to model a huge phallus. He placed this in the clay hand, and Sadakichi rewrapped the ensemble.

"We returned to the company," Decker said, "to have a few more drinks. The sculptress was having some difficulty in persuading her guests to lay off the bootleg booze long enough for the unveiling."

Finally she herded her guests up the stairs to the studio. As they gathered around the veiled object the sculptress explained to them that the love and enthusiasm one must have for artistic success are bound to be reflected in the accomplished masterpiece.

"She became transported as she talked," Decker said. "Then she took hold of the wet hood. 'Now quiet, everybody, please!' she called out. 'I felt truly inspired as I modeled this. And I hope that you will experience the same wonderful thrill when you look upon it.' She removed the cloth but did not immediately look at her handiwork. Instead she studied the faces of her drunken guests as though to catch their first reactions. She scarcely had time to say, 'I call it "The Hand of Friendship,"' when there was hell to pay."

Some of the guests laughed, and others began to buzz among themselves. The sculptress turned to look at her masterwork. "She had a rush of blood to the head," Decker continued, "and might have fallen to the floor; but somebody held her up while a drink was supplied. Sadakichi was all for staying on, but I dragged him away when I heard someone mention the police."

It was during this season in Greenwich Village that Decker challenged Sadakichi to prove his claim that he knew more about the art of picking pockets and snatching purses than did the best professionals. Hartmann volunteered to give a demonstration of his skill outside Wanamaker's.

"Sadakichi picked out a prospective victim," Decker said, "a lady shopper in the crowd that was moving in and out of the department store at the rush hour. He latched onto her handbag, quickly placed it inside his overcoat and cleverly removed the purse. While the victim was standing open-mouthed, looking all around for the robber, Hartmann politely asked her what was wrong. She said someone had taken her handbag. He asked her to identify it, then produced the bag, saying he had chanced to rescue it from the sidewalk. She thanked him and opened the bag, saying she would like to reward him, if only in a small way. She now discovered that her purse was missing. Sadakichi asked how much money there had been in it. She said four dollars. Sadakichi had only three dollars of his own, so he borrowed one from me, then offered the four to the grateful woman. She didn't want to take it, but Sadakichi charmed her into accepting the money."

After she had gone away Sadakichi opened the purse to find but a dollar and seventy-five cents! "I thought he would have apoplexy," Decker said.

Among Decker's and Sadakichi's friends of those days was a talented artist who imagined himself in constant danger of contracting hydrophobia. He would tremble whenever he saw a dog on the street, whether or not the animal was on a leash.

The three friends, Decker, Hartmann, and the rabies-fearing artist, were walking in Washington Square one day when the painter saw a stray poodle coming toward them, wagging its tail. The artist began to tremble violently. Decker helped him to a park bench, scared away the poodle, then asked his friend to try to compose himself.

"Oh my God!" the painter exclaimed. "I'm in agony!"

"Where does it hurt you?" Decker asked.

"It's not physical pain," the artist replied. "I feel like killing myself."

"Now, now," Decker tried to soothe him. "Suppose you tell us."

"I keep thinking I'm going to catch rabies. I know it's absurd. But I'm becoming mad with the fear of it. Can't eat or sleep. What am I to do?"

Decker asked Sadakichi for an opinion. "If more artists committed suicide," Hartmann replied, "we would have less bad art and everybody would be much better off."

Decker reprimanded Sadakichi for this cynicism.

"What would you do if you were in my place?" the artist asked Decker.

"Well," Decker replied, "I'd go right out and deliberately expose myself to every dog in town."

At this, according to Decker, the obsessed artist fell unconscious to the asphalt path. "A policeman came, and I persuaded him that our friend was not drunk. An ambulance took him to the hospital. A doctor there recommended that he undergo psychoanalytic therapy. Our friend's family was well-to-do—a fact that had influenced Sadakichi's interest in him in the first place—and quite able to afford expensive medical care."

The man who feared rabies spent almost a year in couch talk, Decker said. "He had been a successful artist, an exceptionally fine colorist, and especially adroit in painting working people against backgrounds of industrial life. After the psychoanalytical course he completely lost his fear of dogs and of hydrophobia and slept well of nights—but never again managed to paint with his former skill, or with any real conviction, or his onetime originality."

At the conclusion of Decker's story Sadakichi said, "There is a bit of madness in every good artist. If he surrenders it he may be forfeiting a most valuable asset."

Sadakichi decided to return to California after he was arrested in the backyard of a funeral parlor, where he had been gathering material for his brochure on cremation. The undertaker had just given one of his coffins a coat of varnish and had set it outside his establishment to dry in the noonday sun. Sadakichi had seen the coffin from a window of Decker's second-story room. He went to the yard with a bottle of whisky and made himself comfortable in the coffin. The undertaker found him asleep there and called the police.

Matt Moore kept Hartmann out of jail but advised him to leave town at once. Moore was making a great deal of money as a screen actor, working opposite Miss Marion Davies at the Cosmopolitan Studios in New York, and Sadakichi had heard of his good fortune. Hartmann read the newspapers carefully each day and compiled a list of potential benefactors to whom he would write or call on in person, if that were possible.

Moore was known as a "soft touch," so it was not long before Sadakichi sought him out. When he offered to serve as Moore's publicity man the actor bought him a typewriter, which Sadakichi at once pawned.

"Over the years," Moore said recently, "I gave Hartmann thousands of dollars. But I figured I got millions out of him in the laughter he provoked, and in the spectacle of his odd character."

Moore had sublet the New York apartment of screen actress Aileen Pringle, a San Francisco girl who was on a visit to her parents in that western city. Sadakichi had met Miss Pringle in San Francisco and had persuaded some of her wealthy friends to finance a sequel to his quasi-religious book; the new work was entitled *The Last Thirty Days of Christ*. He had dedicated it to Miss Pringle.

"I used to take Hartmann to the Lambs Club," Moore said. "The members would look at him as if he were a man from Mars. The boy at the desk, where you had to register a guest, would ask, 'Mr. Moore, are you sure you want this man to come in with you?' and I'd say, 'Yes, let him in.' "

Some weeks after Sadakichi left New York, Moore received instructions from Miss Pringle to send certain of her personal effects to San Francisco. While gathering together these things Moore discovered that Miss Pringle's first edition of *The Last Thirty Days* was missing. He knew Sadakichi well enough to presume that he had taken the book. The actor received a postal card from Hartmann, who wrote that he had stopped over at an artists' colony at Albuquerque, New Mexico. Moore telegraphed Sadakichi that he presently was going to Hollywood to live and work and advised Hartmann to meet him, with the book, at the Albuquerque railway station during the stopover of the Santa Fe *Chief*.

"Instead of meeting me with the book," Moore continued, "Sadakichi showed up with his luggage. 'Moore,' he said, 'I'm going out to Hollywood with you.' And he did."

For some years thereafter Moore contributed to Sadakichi's support. When the actor bought a place at the sea-
shore Sadakichi promptly invited himself as a house guest.
"I could not let him use any of the bedrooms," Moore said,
"because the stench of his pipe was almost impossible to
get rid of. He slept on a studio couch in the study, and
kept the fireplace going all night, even in the hottest
weather. One day I got rid of all available firewood. Later
on I smelled cloth burning. On investigation I found Sadakichi walking around the place in his underwear. He had
burned his other clothes in the fireplace; and of course I had
to supply him with one of my own suits. Unfortunately my
clothes fitted him, and suits kept disappearing all year
round."

Moore didn't mind it a bit when Sadakichi wanted money
but objected to his acts of kleptomania. "He was very clever.
I had a pair of fine binoculars in a leather case hanging in
my study. One day I wanted to use the glasses for a close
view of a sailing ship but found the case empty.

"Sadakichi used to come to my house with a big suit-
case," Moore went on to say. "I noticed that when he'd
leave, the case would be much heavier than it was when he
arrived. So I said no more suitcases, and he would visit me
with just a briefcase. But you'd be amazed how much stuff
he could get into it—first editions and the like."

One evening Moore invited William Randolph Hearst and
a party of the publisher's friends to go home with him for
a midnight snack. They entered the Moore residence and
snapped on the lights, to find Sadakichi half-naked and

asleep among an array of empty bottles. The publisher wanted no part of this scene. He retired with his companions just as Sadakichi roused to ask if the women members of the party were "concubines."

Moore said that one night in the late 1920s Miss Pringle brought H. L. Mencken to his house. "Sadakichi was staying with me," he continued, "and Mencken greeted him most graciously: 'Sadakichi! After all these years!' Mencken offered Hartmann a job on his magazine. 'You pick out any five contemporary writers,' Mencken said to him, 'and then write articles about them for *The Mercury*. I'll not edit your work any more than I have to, and I'll pay you the maximum rate.'

"Sadakichi replied, 'How much do I get in advance?'

"Mencken was too smart to give him anything in advance," Moore said. "It seems strange that Hartmann had had so many fine jobs offered him at various times in his life. He seldom accepted a job; or, if he did, would do something awful to lose it. It seems he never finished much of anything, except a friendship or a bottle."

Matt Moore is one of the most contented men of my acquaintance. Although his days of stardom and huge earnings are over, his good nature has not altered. Indeed, in the small seaside place to which he moved after living in mansions, he has become even more gracious than before, more understanding of life. The lasting sea sounds the same outside every man's door.

"The last time I saw Sadakichi," Moore told me, "was during World War Two. My little house was in a closely re-

stricted military district. Even I had to identify myself with
a card each time I came in or went out of my home. The
Army had fenced in the neighborhood, put up a gate, and
stationed a guard there. One morning my doorbell and my
telephone rang at the same time. I went to the door first—
a great mistake on my part. The landlady was trying to
warn me by telephone, I afterward learned, that Sadakichi
was at my door.

"How he had got past the guard and through the gate I
never could find out. 'Listen,' I said to Hartmann, 'we are
at war with both Germany and Japan, and you are half of
each. You are bound to be hated both ways, and here you
are in a military zone. They'll kill you and make me move
out of here.'

"Sadakichi serenely replied, 'May I have some breakfast
before the execution?' "

In May of 1941 I decided to go to Tahiti. I had read
about a Matson Line cruise, the first in more than a year to
that island, and I needed a breathing spell. I was fifty-one
years old and wished to decide upon the wisdom of giving up
work that brought in "big money" for work of my own
choice and enjoyment.

Perhaps a conversation I had with Barrymore influenced
me. Although I seldom have referred to our more serious
moments, it should not be supposed that my friends and
I neglected to speak of realistic matters or failed to discuss
among ourselves the more solemn aspects of life.

"Just what do you think you are doing?" Barrymore asked

me one day. His manner was quite serious. When I did not reply at once he added, "You know well enough what I mean."

"First," I replied, "suppose you tell me what *you* are doing?"

He spoke slowly and with an air of sadness. "I am doing the work of a whore."

"Indeed?"

"By necessity—or so it would seem—I am occupied with what is loosely called 'Radio,' and an occasional frothy picture. I have been told that no one will lock me up if I earn big money—money that nobody but my creditors gets. So I do it. And I find it the work of a whore." He looked at me, or rather, through me. "There is nothing as sad in all the world as an *old* prostitute. I think that every artist somewhere along the line should know what it is to be one, a *young* one, but reform. Please, my friend, don't keep on working in pictures, where you most certainly don't find any real satisfaction. Get out now!"

On the voyage to Tahiti I decided to say good-by, as soon as my commitment expired the next year, to work that too often made me feel like an embezzler. I was in this work, but never quite *of* it. I did not then, and do not now, look down on the good work that sometimes is done on the screen. There are many gifted, sincere men and women engaged in that work. It was simply that I could not in all decency continue to be enormously overpaid in terms of money for something I was not fitted to do, and in the way I was asked to do it: on call.

There springs to mind a remembrance of one picture

producer who asked me on a day long ago, "Why do you neglect your work at the studio to take care of a drunken has-been like Barrymore?" I was too old to hit anyone on the chin, so I replied, "Barrymore is the most remarkable personality I know, both as a man and as a genius. Also he is my friend."

The next time I saw this producer was at Romanoff's restaurant. Some ten years had passed. He seemed shrunken, empty of life, and unhappy. An old whore.

FIFTEEN

Would joy prove a more steady guest
In palm-girt summer southern lands?
Some lambent world of green and gold?
　　　　　　　—Sadakichi

Many sea-miles away from Bundy Drive, I thought of my friends at Decker's studio. They were extraordinary men, vital and forthright, and each had within himself great staying powers. Clocks run down. Men run down. You can rewind a clock. What hand is there so cunning as to wind up a man?

From a doorway that looks seaward I watch a Polynesian woman as she alternately wades, then floats face-down, in the spending surf. She makes use of a wooden box, crudely fashioned, with a pane of glass on the bottom, to peer beneath the surface of the water in search of sea urchins. She has on a cerise calico garment and a fisherman's black hat, the brim upturned from her placid face. The glass-bottomed crate can accommodate both her head and the hat as she submerges the homemade device part way in the backwash of the tide. Each time she bends over, her rump comes up like a pan of new bread dough. She catches a sea urchin with her deft bare hands, then places it in a cloth sack suspended from a cord looped about her waist.

At sundown she comes ashore. Her man puts the sea urchins in a dry burlap sack and shakes them till the spines are rubbed free. Then they have a feast upon the fresh, sweet meat. They drink palm wine, sing, make love, then sleep. Their lives appear to be uncomplicated and serene, concerned neither with yesterday nor tomorrow. They seek, and they find.

When you are far away you think of many things that escaped your consideration while you were moving among the possessive clamors of an accustomed scene. Perhaps now you clearly remember a word that, at the time of its utterance, had seemed of little consequence; or you may recall a friend's smile, or a woman's tear, or an injury done to someone once dear to you. Quite suddenly there springs to mind the recollection of a carelessly dealt-with hour, one that—in the unwelcome memory of it—makes you feel as though you had played with a gun you had not known was loaded.

I remembered something Barrymore had said on one of the few occasions he chanced to speak about his own pattern of life: "My mind dreamed up miracles impossible to reach in lived fact. Actors do that; and I suppose that is why they make such unsatisfactory husbands. I've done everything three times; the fourth time around becomes monotonous."

And W. C. Fields had said: "If I showed too much eager-

ness now, the bastards would expect me to grab the brass
ring every time. What would I be proving?"

And Decker had said: "We are too big for our bodies. We
spring the seams, then blow to pieces."

Our synthetic hero, Sadakichi—the only one among us
who howled against fate like a muezzin calling from the
minaret of a crumbling mosque—had denounced me for re-
fusing to see life as anything other than a great hoax, with
all men the victims of some monstrous practical joke.

Not that I accepted the good-fairy pap, offered by the
lesser Brownings, that all was well with the world; but I
was too enamored of life to think the living of it futile.
Seeing, breathing, hearing, the smell of life—I interpreted
these as valid evidence that the house I resided in, though
not always kept in good repair, had been leased to me on
fair terms by a most lenient Landlord.

I returned from Tahiti late in June 1941 to find my friends
in various degrees of personal turmoil but still in the ring,
as the saying is. There were a few changes to be remarked
in and about the studio. The vines Decker had planted to
screen his backyard from his neighbors had become a colorful jungle—he was an amazingly successful gardener. There
were two new dogs, and a new cat that played with all of
Decker's dogs on even terms. There was a small parrot that
sat on Decker's shoulder as he painted or played chess with
Barrymore. A new whitewashed split-rail fence, built by
the artist, enclosed the front yard. And an avocado tree's
roots had wrestled with the cesspool and won, with the re-
sult that no one could rely upon the studio plumbing. But

the friends who gathered there on Bundy Drive were the same; and the smell of the turpentine was the same; and Phyllis was, as always, beautiful and kind.

The ceiling of Decker's kitchen still bore the blue-green splotches, but the walls and the cabinet doors had been redecorated. Because of Decker's diabetes, the half-starved lover of fine food decided to feast his eyes if not his belly. He had selected from various magazines an array of colored advertisements, all having to do with edibles. He had scissored out pictures of bread, pork chops, cutlets, steaks, roasts, bacon, hams, salads, pastries, dressings, fish of many kinds, oysters, fruits, berries—anything that would please the palate, and with Phyllis had spent many hours arranging these cut-outs on the kitchen walls.

Decker had also painted a mural to fill in the space above and in back of the stove. It showed a chef, white-hatted and in starched apron, holding a skillet in which a nude young woman lay, sunnyside up.

We had a suitable reunion, of course, and Decker took great pains—in every sense of the word—to cook an excellent dinner, with a joint of veal as the principal meat dish.

"We killed a fatted calf," he explained, drooling as he basted the meat. "Something appropriate to welcome home the prodigal son. Oh, if I could sneak just one little bite of it!"

At table that evening Sadakichi denounced me for having left him summarily to go on a pleasure cruise. W. C. Fields dropped in after dinner, and he accused me of secretly having written a book on Hartmann, a matter he described as "digging your own grave with a quill."

At this Sadakichi waved his hand derisively. Uncle Claude asked him, "Are you umpiring a ball game?"

"Hah!" said Hartmann.

"Hah yourself!" replied W. C. "In fact, a double hah! And also drat!"

Barrymore arrived with Big Karl Stuevers. He said he wanted nothing to eat but could be compelled to take something to drink. He appeared happy to see me, but apparently had forgotten that I had been away for several weeks. He was becoming more and more oblivious to recent events. For example, he gave his dachshund Gus to Decker, and then next day saw the dog at the artist's house and heard someone call him "Gus." "I used to have a dog named Gus," he said.

At tonight's get-together artist Henry Clive performed several of his card tricks. During his youth in Australia, Clive had been on the vaudeville stage as a sleight-of-hand artist. When someone, that night at Decker's, charged that Clive had a confederate among us, he called on Gus the dachshund to assist him with the next trick. Incredible as it may seem, Gus chose a card from Clive's fanned-out deck, then ran out of the room with it in his mouth. During the dog's absence from the room Clive named the card as the queen of diamonds. Gus thereupon reappeared with the card still in his mouth, and we saw that it indeed was the queen.

Barrymore proposed that we attend the gala opening of John Murray Anderson's cabaret, where Decker had painted the murals. During the last two weeks of Decker's work there Barrymore had sat alternately watching him and the rehearsing girls. Whenever Decker observed that Jack was getting interested in one of the chorus girls the artist would slyly draw a caricature of that girl and show it to Jack, who would say, "Hmm. I see what you mean." And once again he would be saved from getting into trouble. Or, as Phyllis Decker said, "The girl was saved."

Barrymore insisted that we dress formally for the occasion. I sent Karl to my house for a tuxedo, and Decker got out his dinner coat. Fields announced he would not dress for this or any other event short of being made a Knight of the Garter. He said that he would meet us later on at the cabaret—in tweeds.

Decker and I presently left with Jack, who said he had to stop over at his brother Lionel's former residence in Beverly Hills to borrow some evening clothes. Lionel now was living in Chatsworth, but still maintained the house where he and his late wife Irene Fenwick had lived. He would neither sell nor lease this place, but kept it furnished as it had been, and left Mrs. Barrymore's belongings, as well as some of his own clothes, undisturbed. The pictures Lionel had painted stayed on the walls of this house, and his books upon the library shelves. A housekeeper lived on the premises, and a watchdog guarded the backyard. Lionel sometimes visited this house to sit there alone with his memories.

The faithful housekeeper had gone for the day when we arrived at the shrine. Jack climbed the driveway gate; and, notwithstanding his usual success with animals, the watchdog promptly nipped him in the backside.

"He knows I'm a thief," Jack said as he let us in the gate. "And worse still, he sees me as a relative!"

Decker found an unlocked window, entered by way of it,

then unlatched the kitchen door for us. The telephone had been ringing the while.

"Don't answer it," Decker warned, but Barrymore had a mind very much his own.

"Hello," he said into the instrument. "No, I'm very sorry, sir. You can't speak to the housekeeper. Why not? I'll tell you precisely why not, my inquisitive friend: because that lady is right beside me in bed, and I can't spare her absence even for one instant."

Jack turned to us. "He hung up on me!"

He showed us upstairs to Lionel's former bedroom, where he raided the wardrobe for a suit of black tails, a stiff-bosomed shirt, a white waistcoat, a wing collar, white tie, a set of cuff-links and studs.

"Unfortunately," he said, "I am wearing brown bedroom slippers, and Lionel's shoes don't fit me. How inconsiderate of him! Uncle John Drew's boots were exactly my size."

Lionel was taller and much larger of chest than his brother. In the borrowed evening clothes Jack looked like a minstrel man. We found some safety pins, rubber bands, paperclips, and a piece of string, and used these articles to cinch in our friend's finery. He was delighted and promised to get jobs for us with the tailors' guild.

At the John Murray Anderson première Barrymore mischievously proposed marriage to Mae West. She enjoyed his sallies and replied in kind. A gentleman at a nearby table, however, frowned upon the whole thing and asked Barrymore to censor his language; whereupon Jack foretold that the man soon would be paying huge alimony. As a matter of fact, the prophecy came true some months later.

We had a fine time of it, and Fields suggested we do it again sometime—"say in about ninety years."

That night, after everyone else had gone on home, Big Karl drove Decker, Jack, and me to Bundy Drive. The artist suddenly seemed very melancholy.

I asked if he was ill, and he replied, "I'm in trouble."

"Have you not read in Holy Writ," said Barrymore, "that man born of woman is of few days, and full of trouble?"

Decker stared at a bottle of cognac. "Diabetes or no diabetes, I feel like hitting the booze."

Barrymore placed a hand on his friend's shoulder. "Look here, old man, what is it? Creditors? Dames?"

I kept no immediate detailed notes of this occasion and must rely as best I can upon my recollection of what Decker told us, in confidence. In effect he said that if the United States entered World War II—and that seemed inevitable— he would be called upon by the authorities to explain his status as an alien.

At first we thought he was talking merely to hear himself, but he went on to say that his real name was Leopold Wolfgang von der Decken, the son of the late Baron von der Decken. His father had been a colonel of the Prussian Guards, and had met his San Francisco-born mother at the Berlin Opera, when she was singing contralto roles in the *Ring des Nibelungen.* He had followed her to the Bayreuth Festival and married her against the wishes of his titled father.

"When I was but two years old," Decker told us, "my father and mother took me to live in Brixton, Surrey, England. My father became a London newspaper correspondent for the *Berliner Tagblatt,* and I grew up hating both of them, especially my mother. I went to school for a time, then as a kid worked with Joseph Harker, the famous London scenic artist."

I received, at a much later time, full confirmation of this part of Decker's story, in a letter from his boyhood playmate, John Bonstall of Surrey, England. Mr. Bonstall said that the title of baron was inherited by Decker when the father died in 1936. That title went back to the time of the Franco-Prussian War, when Decker's grandfather, then a forester residing on the Franco-Prussian border, gave sanctuary to a German general and received the title from the Kaiser.

Decker told Barrymore and me that his parents quarreled, separated, then left him to shift for himself in 1908 or 1909. While he was working as an apprentice among the lofts of the painter of theatrical scenery, he was approached by a Dickensian sort of man who offered to befriend him. This man revealed, cautiously at first, a way for Decker to better his miserable circumstances.

The Good Samaritan, according to Decker's story, was one of the most successful art forgers in the world. He was an elderly man, with the appearance and manner of a curate. He made his living by painting supposedly genuine works of dead masters and selling them to American tourists.

The unscrupulous master and the adolescent boy would prowl about in out-of-the-way places in search of worm-eaten wood, half-rotted canvas, and other aged materials upon which to paint their frauds. The old fellow was too sharp to copy a well-known work, Decker said; instead he imitated the style of artists of repute.

"Now you can see," Decker said, "how easy it is for me to reproduce a Van Gogh or a Gauguin." For that matter, Decker could perform ably in the style of Rouault, Utrillo, Modigliani, and others.

Van Gogh was the artistic love of Decker's life, then and always. He would steal materials from his crooked bene-factor, and, alone in his cheap room in a London flat, work in the style of the Dutch painter.

One day in 1916 Decker heard a knocking at his door. "I opened it" (and I am remembering Decker's words as best I can) "to see a heavily built man of middle age. He had a red beard and looked like photographs I had seen of King Edward VII. He spoke English with a trace of German ac-cent. He came in and admired the pictures I had painted in the Van Gogh manner, some of them relatively small in size. Naturally I was more than pleased, for praise and money seldom came my way. He offered me ten pounds for four of the smaller pictures."

The bearded stranger paid him in pound notes. The now affluent young artist set out to enjoy his first extended fling at romance—and stayed away from his job and his flat for three days.

When he had spent the money Decker returned to his quarters to paint several more Van Goghs. After a week or so the bearded man called again. The stranger said he had liked Decker's work so much he was prepared to buy six paintings. John doubled the price.

The artist immediately went out to find another sweetheart; but first he put aside half his new wealth in a bank account. That was the last time he ever would trust a bank.

His address was found in the bank records by Scotland Yard; and when Decker got home he was arrested by two officers and put in the Tower of London.

"The red-bearded man also was arrested," Decker went on to say. "We were tried at the same time as German spies. My customer had taken my pictures, put an extra canvas on the back of each one, and on the shielded back of each picture had written espionage information in code—something to do with ships. Three of these paintings were intercepted before they could be smuggled to Sweden. The man was sentenced to death. Because of my youth, and the doubt as to my actual connection with a spy ring, I was spared the death sentence and was interned on the Isle of Man for the duration. And maybe my bad luck with those canvases was one of the main reasons I'd rather paint on board."

Decker spent two years behind electrified barbed wire on the Isle of Man, an experience that warped his views on life. "I saw too much," he said, "and learned too much—most of it degrading. Only when I paint or drink can I forget it even now."

Because of the German blockade, with the consequent food shortage for everyone, the prisoners subsisted on a diet mostly of fish. There was no butter, no sugar. And it was on the Isle of Man that Decker looked each evening at the setting sun and came to hate it.

There was one old internee, Decker said, a sweet-tem-

pered German toymaker. The other prisoners grew tired of
his oft-repeated stories about the happier days in the Father-
land and wearied of his references to his wonderful son and
how the boy surely one day would write to him or perhaps
come to see him at the stockade. One prisoner, bored by the
old man's prattle, seized a frayed photograph of the son
from the father's hands and tore it to bits. The father wept
all that day.

Decker listened patiently to the old man's daydreams,
to the endless stories of the son's virtues. "One day in the
prison yard" (and again I must rely upon my memory of
Decker's long-ago recital), "perhaps a year after this old
toymaker had begun to await word from his son, a guard
brought a young man to the stockade. When the old man
saw this youngster he turned pale. 'I told you! I told you
he'd come!' the old man kept crying out, and he staggered
over to greet the young man. It didn't seem to cross the
poor old guy's mind that his boy was a fellow prisoner, not
a caller.

"The son just stood there glaring at his father, not making
a move. When the old man opened his arms to embrace his
son the young fellow began to curse him. It was terrible.
He blamed his father for his arrest, saying that the letters
written by the old man had been intercepted and had in-
criminated him. He spat in the old man's face. And then,
my God! the feeble old fellow stood as if stunned by a
sudden blow. After a few moments he got some kind of
weird strength. He turned, ran, and threw himself against
the high-voltage wire. He shook in a great spasm. He did
not scream. His body turned halfway around, then hung

there against the wire and the setting sun, like God on the Cross."

After the war Decker was released. He went to Germany, Italy, and then to France, where he became acquainted with Modigliani. One of that artist's group forged a passport to enable Decker to go to America as a returned citizen, ostensibly a native of San Francisco.

"Now," Decker said, "you can see what will hang over me when the United States declares war on Germany. They'll dig up my record, and nobody will think me anything but an enemy and a spy."

"You should tell your story to someone in authority right away," I said. "That's the best thing for you to do, regardless."

Perhaps he did get in touch with a Washington official, an important man who had admired his work. However, when war came to America that December, the artist seemed soul-weary and apprehensive. He frequently forgot about his diabetes and drank heavily.

At the beginning of the war, when the older men were called upon to register for home defense, Decker seemed most reluctant to sign up. I insisted that he comply with the order. The humorous incident that occurred at the registration headquarters compensated for any fears he may have had at the time.

The registration was intended for men above draft age, and younger than sixty. W. C. Fields had passed sixty but— vain old boy that he was—insisted upon going with us.

Decker was but forty-five. I was fifty-one, and Barrymore would soon be sixty.

I must say that we seemed a bedraggled foursome as we arrived at the place of registration, somewhere in Santa Monica. Barrymore's swollen legs had been giving him trouble. Decker's diabetes had made him as thin, almost, as Sadakichi. I was still somewhat bent over from the automobile accident of two years ago, and walked with a stick. Fields looked like the wrath of John Barleycorn. His nose had on it a piece of courtplaster to shield a broken blister suffered from too much exposure to the sun. He was fair of complexion, and when he had fallen asleep on the open deck of a fishing boat off Catalina Island the sun's heat had been too much for his already inflamed nose.

A sweet-faced young woman gave us the necessary forms to fill out for home defense. As she did so she put us back on our heels with the question, "Gentlemen, who sent you? The enemy?"

There is no answer to the quest.
Who knows when we'll meet again?
—Sadakichi

Phyllis Decker paid more attention than we did to our respective birthdays. She reminded us that John Barrymore would be sixty on February 15, 1942, and suggested having a gala celebration.

The fact that Jack would soon be sixty did not seem to agree, somehow, with our conception of his personality. It seemed almost incredible to us that this young-at-heart man, gifted beyond measure in talent and in bodily vigor, could ever grow old. True, he sometimes looked tired, or bloated, and ready, as he put it, to climb into his urn. Then, quite unexpectedly, he would rouse, regain his spirits, take on a semblance of health—thus confuting the polka-dot thinking of Hollywood critics, whom he scorned—and resume the playing of the grand opera that was his life.

Upon learning of Barrymore's vanished sixty years Decker said to him, "What are your plans for the second half of your life?"

"I shall spend it at sea. The skipper of the *Flying Dutchman* is signing me on as a boatswain."

Barrymore actually was born on St. Valentine's Day, February 14, 1882, as I learned when I obtained a copy of his birth certificate in Philadelphia, in the course of checking source material for my book *Good Night, Sweet Prince.* Jack, as well as some other members of his family, assumed that the fifteenth instead of the fourteenth of February was his birth date. Not that he cared much when he was born.

He had been ill many times this past year and presently was recovering from a severe cold, but was on hand for the party. He arrived at the studio while Phyllis was telephoning W. C. Fields to ask that he join us. The comedian declined the invitation politely but definitely.

Uncle Claude spoke against all holidays, anniversaries, or feast days, with the single exception of April First. Phyllis thought I might prevail upon W. C. to come to the party; but when I got on the telephone I received his customary evasive answer.

"And you can do it in spades!" he added.

Also absent from the studio that evening was Sadakichi Hartmann. Since the United States declaration of war in December the old fellow had not wandered far from the Indian reservation. Decker said he hoped our half-Japanese, half-German friend would stay right where he was and practice his war whoops and snake dances far from Bundy Drive.

"He's bound to pop in here sometime though." Decker sighed. "And then we'll both land in the pokey for keeps."

"Let us telephone the Bard of Nippon," Barrymore suggested. "Perhaps he has composed a new sonnet."

"Hell no!" shouted Decker. "Anyway, there's no telephone in his wigwam."

"We could send up smoke signals," Jack said, "and he could answer us by using his pipe."

Decker unveiled a recently completed portrait of Earl Carroll. The former producer of Broadway musical shows now operated a large restaurant in Hollywood, where a musical revue was to be seen twice each night. Barrymore frequently attended the rehearsals, where he was made much of by the producer as well as by the ladies of the ensemble. He invited us to go to Carroll's for the birthday party.

During the midnight show Jack left the table to go to the gentlemen's washroom. By some mischance he wandered into the ladies' rest room. Everyone there—except Jack—seemed slightly embarrassed by this intrusion.

A woman customer took him to task just as he was emerging from a booth of convenience. "Don't you know this is for ladies?" she said sharply.

He bowed courteously. "Yes, madam. And so am I."

Later an usher handed Barrymore a note from comedian Jack Oakie. The note contained birthday greetings, as well as a friendly suggestion that Barrymore's pet Afghan bitch Viola be bred to one of the comedian's prize-winning hounds. Oakie's Afghan kennels were considered the best on the Pacific Coast.

Upon reading this note Barrymore became so furious that

I thought it best to take him at once to his Tower Road home. He threatened to kill Oakie on sight.

Perhaps this incident calls for some explanation. The mention of Viola for motherhood triggered the actor's pent-up grievances against anyone and everyone whom he fancied had stripped him not only of worldly possessions but also of his chances for happiness. Viola was the last of his long line of assorted pets. He had acquired the graceful creature from Fanny Brice a year or so before and had become quite attached to the animal, and it to him.

The first time Barrymore saw Viola, Miss Brice was not at home, but her young daughter Frances was, and Jack insisted that she sell him the animal, with or without her mother's consent.

Frances thought things over and said she would have to get at least fifty dollars for Viola.

"I don't have fifty dollars on my person," Barrymore explained. "No one trusts me, so let us not break the chain."

A day or so went by, and Jack reappeared at Fanny Brice's. No one was at home but the servants. He put forty-seven dollars in the butler's hand. "Tell Brice I only had forty-seven dollars, and she's damned lucky to get that much from me."

After the birthday party, as Jack was getting into a bathrobe at his Tower Road home he picked up Jack Oakie's note, which had fallen to the floor. He reread it, then once again went into a tirade. I tried to persuade him that Oakie was a most amiable person and that his reference to Viola's visit to his kennels had been innocently intended.

"Innocent!" he shouted, gathering Viola in his arms. To

the best of my recollection, he then said, "Damn anyone who has an eye on this pet of mine! She's all I have left. They've taken everything from me. I've let the greedy bastards strip me and exploit me. Not satisfied with that, they saw to it that I lost every living thing that loved me or that I loved. Now they'd take Viola, and put her through pain, and maybe death. She's getting old and would die, just as every other thing I've ever loved has been stolen or is dead."

I induced Jack to take a sleeping pill and drink some warm milk, then sat beside his bed while he slept uneasily for perhaps two hours. Viola lay across the foot of the bed; she opened her kind eyes each time her master stirred.

When Jack awakened at daybreak he wanted to return to Decker's studio. We found the artist at his easel. He was painting a ghost-town scene, one of a series that had been occupying his artistic attention off and on for the last month or so. He had interrupted this work only to paint Earl Carroll. He said of him, "Carroll is getting to look more and more like a ghost, so it all adds up."

The smell of food cooking in the kitchen drifted in to us. Decker was preparing sausages and frying potatoes for his breakfast—and to hell with diabetes!

"Wonderful!" Barrymore said. "Precisely what I'd like to devour."

We were delighted that Barrymore was hungry. Too often he had declined to eat anything at all, day or night. Decker cheerfully surrendered his breakfast to Jack and placed it on a coffee table beside the chair that once had belonged to Valentino. Barrymore ate the sausages and potatoes with much relish, while Decker went to the kitchen to prepare another breakfast.

Barrymore fell asleep in his chair. Some twenty minutes later he awakened, smelled the food being cooked, and once again called out that he was hungry. Decker and I exchanged glances. It had become more apparent to us each day that our friend's memory of recent happenings was rapidly becoming worse.

Decker went to the kitchen, put both his and my intended breakfasts on one large plate, and served the double portion to Jack. The actor ate greedily. "Wonderful!" he said and fell asleep again.

Less than a month afterward, on my own fifty-second birthday, I fell ill with influenza. Barrymore made a private recording of a poem I had written to amuse him, "The Cowboy's Lament," and sent it to me as a birthday present, together with a note:

> Dear Bret Harte: As one of the outcasts of Poker Flat (wanted in four states for indecent exposure) I send you greetings. Your poem is infinitely superior to any of the Bard's soliloquies. I am instituting the first steps looking toward your beatification. Sainthood will follow in due course. Please promise me never to reform.

In April I received a telephone call from a worried Decker. "Sadakichi is at my studio! Says he's not Japanese at all, but has just discovered that his mother was a Korean!"

Decker tried to explain to the obdurate Hartmann that by his mere presence he was placing everyone in the household in jeopardy.

"Just as I thought," Hartmann said. "I am a man unwanted."

He told Decker that earlier in the day he had been standing at a Banning street intersection when a passing motorist stopped to ask directions. Sadakichi said he was a stranger himself to the town—a lie of course—then asked for a lift.

"Where do you want to go?" the man asked.

"Anywhere," Sadakichi replied. "Wherever I go, there I will find Destiny awaiting me with the laurel leaves."

"I'd like to find the shortest route to Los Angeles," the motorist said. "Get in, and we'll ask someone the way."

Upon reaching Hollywood the motorist refused to take Hartmann farther than Vine Street. The old fellow got into a taxicab to go the remaining ten miles of his journey to Decker's; and the artist, of course, had to supply the fare. The self-appointed Korean demanded food, drink, and some phonograph music. He would not leave until Decker had made a descent to the cellar to get a fifty-dollar bill from the pirate's chest and had telephoned for a taxicab to call for the unwelcome guest.

Even then Hartmann was in no hurry to depart and kept the taxicab standing outside Decker's door for almost an hour. When I appeared on the scene Hartmann greeted me with a sarcastic speech. Then he delivered a lecture, but I can recall only this part of it. "Decker keeps hammering at me to approve his art. Hah! Painters often forget that the soul alone can speak to the soul; and the soul of painting—not its form—is lasting."

Soon after this a bright-mannered young man from Military Intelligence called on me. I showed him to my study.

He displayed his card of authority. "Do you know a man named Sadakichi Hartmann?"

"Indeed I do."

"Would you care to tell me what you know about him?"

"Have you a month or so to spend as my guest?"

The young man studied me for a time. "Does he hate America?"

"He hates the whole world."

"Oh?" My visitor seemed a bit concerned. "I have been assigned to make inquiries about him. This is confidential, of course. Does he oppose this war?"

"He opposes all war."

"He does?"

"Yes, and so did General Grant. You will find in Grant's *Memoirs* that he regarded the Mexican War as a most unworthy action of conquest, and the War between the States as a terrible tragedy."

After a silence I said to the young man, "I take it that you are trying to determine whether, because of Hartmann's German-Japanese ancestry, he is a dangerous person these days?"

"That, and the circumstances of his arrest in the First World War. Do you think he might possibly be working against the present war effort?"

"He is a very old man, and ill," I said. "And I don't think anyone would trust him with a mission, good or bad. Suppose I let you read my correspondence with him? It will take some time to do so, but I think it will afford you a true measure of his character. Then I'll answer all your questions."

The young man occupied himself for some two or three hours with the Sadakichi letters and papers. Meantime I did my garden chores.

Almost an acre of vacant ground stood next to my house, and there I had planted a flower garden that had grown into a "project." I had patterned the beds in the form of an artist's palette. When viewed from a hillside to the north of my home the flowers looked like blobs of paint on a huge palette.

While I was busy in my garden a family of tourists in a drive-yourself automobile stopped near the place I was weeding. The spokesman of this party, obviously a person used to having his orders carried out, called to me, "Come here, my man."

I took off my hat, an old and almost defunct pith helmet from Egypt, and went over to the car. "Yes, sir? May I help you?"

He nodded toward my house. "Does Lana Turner live here?"

In a courteous tone I replied, "If Lana Turner did live here, sir, do you think I'd be outdoors?"

The gentleman drove off, puzzled. The other members of his party kept looking back at me, as if hoping I never would get an old-age pension. I returned inside the house to find that my young caller had completed his inspection.

He asked with a tone of much interest, "And you *like* this man?"

"I think the world of him."

"But he can't be a very pleasant character."

"I never ask that anyone be pleasant to me. All that I seek in a man is native intelligence and integrity in his thinking."

I have not seen this young man again, but I should like to think he has gone far in whatever work he has chosen to pursue. For he displayed a quick understanding.

He shook hands cordially with me. "We shall write Mr. Hartmann down as 'harmless,'" he said.

"Good," I replied. "But be sure not to let him know you call him that."

The month of May came, and with it a great sorrow. Barrymore, while on his way to a radio broadcast, fell ill, then collapsed at the studio.

Earlier that day I had telephoned to ask him how he was feeling. "I feel like hell," he had said. "That's precisely how I feel."

Lionel Barrymore, Decker, and I remained at the Hollywood Hospital while Jack made his last stand. He stayed alive for ten days after his collapse. At ten-thirty o'clock on the night of May 29, 1942, he died.

What is there to add to that which already has been said of this man? In the book I wrote about him I tried to describe his great natural abilities, and spoke of his electric presence on the stage, where he had been the most compelling actor since Booth, and possibly the greatest Hamlet of all time. He didn't merely play that role. Whether on or off the stage, he was Hamlet.

During Jack's last illness the Afghan Viola waited patiently, as if listening for his footsteps or his voice. Lionel eventually took Viola to the shrine in Beverly Hills. The animal escaped one day; then, in the normal course, became the mother of seven puppies, all bitches, and of Great Dane descent on their father's side.

SEVENTEEN

Tell me what name beseems
These vain and wandering days?
—Sadakichi

The morning after Barrymore died Sadakichi telephoned from Banning. At first I was not disposed to talk to
him. I had not been to bed all night or eaten breakfast.
Besides, I would be late for an executors' meeting at which
Jack's will was to be read.

I decided to forgo shaving and a cold shower to accept
Hartmann's call, thinking of course that he meant to speak
of Jack's death.

Nothing of the sort. While I was turning over in my tired
mind what, if anything, I should say to him were he resolved
to run the roadblock of wartime watchers for Japanese, good
or bad, he announced, "I am still of the opinion that Holbein was left-handed."

"What the hell are you talking about?" I asked.

As nearly as I can recall this conversation—for, as I say,
I was tired, and the whisky of the long night had done

nothing for me that it should have—well, I think our conversation ran about as follows.

"When I say something about art or an artist," he muttered, "I do not need to supply proof. I am an authority. Thank you very much."

"Sadakichi, make it snappy, will you?" I said. "Jack is dead, and I have to attend to several things. You should know that."

"When Decker offered his puny arguments," Hartmann persisted, "I supposed at the time that he knew I was talking of Hans Holbein the Younger. And I repeat now what I said: Holbein was left-handed."

For a moment or so I thought I was indeed drunk and having an aural version of the willies. "All right then," I agreed. "Holbein was left-handed. So were Queen Victoria and Babe Ruth. And I don't give a damn if he painted with his feet!"

"You are being difficult," he said. "Or were you asleep as usual when I gave my opinion on Holbein? Hah!"

I managed to recall the scene to which he was referring. There had been a spirited argument at Decker's the day of Hartmann's last visit. Sadakichi had described a self-portrait by the sixteenth-century master as sure evidence of his left-handedness. That self-portrait, Hartmann had said, showed the artist holding his brush in the left hand. Decker had countered with the remark that artists commonly used mirrors when painting their own portraits, and that the reversed image in the mirror would make the right hand seem the left.

"And now," Sadakichi was saying to me over the telephone, "I clearly remember the way the ink strokes ran in the many pen-drawings Holbein made for Erasmus's *Praise of Folly*."

"Sadakichi," I said, "don't you know Jack is dead? And I don't care if Holbein was left-handed, or if Raphael had a harelip, or if Homer was a nance. If you need money, say so, and I'll send it as soon as I can."

I am ashamed to say that I hung up on the old man, for I was genuinely angry with him for not mentioning Barrymore.

On the way to the meeting at Lionel's house I realized belatedly that Sadakichi had been covering up, in a manner of speaking; and by means of his cynical show of indifference at the death of a friend had meant to conceal a real sense of personal loss. That had been his deportment at the time the artist's widow was killed by an automobile after she had dined with him. That had always been his way.

The members of the Bundy Drive group put on no grim masks when a friend died. We would speak of things unrelated to the grief at hand, and sometimes offer a pretended laughter, though it tasted as bitter as a child's first lie. It was our custom always to keep our sorrows to ourselves. Our jests might easily have been, and probably were, misunderstood by strangers to our ways. Whether our lack of long-faced show, on this or other occasions of the same sad measure, sprang from a sense of pride or from some nameless defiance or hidden dread of the last fall of the black curtain—this I cannot know.

At Lionel's Beverly Hills house, the shrine, he showed me a telegram from the New York theatrical producer Arthur Hopkins. This long-time friend of all three Barrymores had years ago given over his stage to Jack's *Richard III* and *Hamlet*. He had known the actor well, both the artist and the man. His wire said:

No, Jack could never bear a part after he grew tired of it. Am sure he has been weary of the last one for a long time. Am glad he has found a new one.

The executors named by John Barrymore to administer his estate were attorney Gordon W. Levoy, Lionel, and I. Although the reading of the will was a legal requirement, it seemed an ironical much-ado about next-to-nothing.

The man who had made three million dollars in his time died with but sixty cents in the clothes he had worn to the hospital. Any things of worth that remained at Tower Road (and the hillside mansion had been sacked of its treasures), together with the house and grounds, upon which rare trees thirsted, were to be auctioned off to satisfy income-tax liens.

When a circus tent is struck late in the night, the carnival moves on to another town. The scavengers come early the next morning to try their luck among the leavings at the fun-deserted scene: they poke solemnly in the trodden saw-dust for stray peanuts, or perhaps a lost coin, or a wrinkled balloon cast aside by some tired child. As the young at-torney read the Barrymore will I sat thinking of Jack's life as a circus that had moved on in the night.

Lionel's housekeeper put a sandwich beside me, but my appetite was off duty. The will seemed endlessly dull to the ear of a professional writer, and quite out of keeping with the character of the man whose every action had been most unprosaic, whose spirit had ever been on the wing.

The will had been drawn at a time when Jack imagined that he possessed many things; not only money and fame, but such prized objects as the marble bust by sculptor Paul Manship and the crayon sketch an aging John Singer Sargent had made for him long ago in Boston; and the many other reminders of those bright brief days when, as the first actor of his time, John Barrymore had ridden across the theatrical sky in a chariot drawn by the horses of the sun.

The voice of the lawyer cut through my thoughts. He was reading a clause of the will that seemed to be, in view of the circumstances, quite futile. Anyone who attacked the provisions of this testament, this clause solemnly warned, would be cut off with but a dollar.

"Just a moment, gentlemen," I interrupted. "Where are we to find the dollar?"

Decker and I had some difficulty persuading Fields to serve as a pallbearer at Barrymore's funeral. "The time to carry a pal," he said, "is when he's still alive."

We called on W. C. very early the morning of the burial. Uncle Claude was still in his bed. Of late he had found it expedient to sleep in a bed with slatted sides, to keep from falling out during the night. It actually was a huge crib; and lying there in his nightclothes he resembled nothing so much as a wicked baby.

"The kind that Daumier would have drawn," Decker said. "The child Gargantua."

"Why should I hoist a graveyard box?" Fields said. "Sure, I was Jack's friend. What's that got to do with it?"

"Well, in case it gets dark," the sardonic Decker said, "your nose would make an excellent tail light."

Fields did not relish jokes about his nose. He would make public sport of it himself during a performance, or permit fellow actors to use it as a target in their dialogue, but he resented any private reference to it. Robert Lewis Taylor points out in his story of Fields that the comedian once took me to task for having reported that his nose had exploded in the sun.

"You are making fun of an affliction," he had said on that occasion. He now repeated the remark to Decker, and his lips were as tight as an oboe player's, a sign of his strong disapproval.

We finally got his promise to be at the funeral. He refused, however, to go with us in the black limousine supplied by the undertaker, in which we had come to his house. He said he didn't like black except when playing roulette, and would go to Calvary Cemetery in his own automobile.

"Besides," he added, "I have some necessary tonics in my car. I am a highly civilized man."

After the requiem mass in the chapel at the cemetery, when the vault was about to be sealed with a marble facing, Fields whispered in my ear, "Don't be a sucker. Come with me in my car. Let's blow."

A large crowd, on hand to see the arrival and the departure of motion-picture celebrities, stood behind a rope barrier across the way from the chapel. As W. C. and I went to his car a throng of noisy young autograph seekers slipped under the rope and descended upon Mr. Fields. The irascible comedian not only did not like to sign pads or papers thrust upon him; he looked upon all persons who asked for his signature as low-browed enemies.

"Get away from me, you little bastards!" he called out to one and all. "For two cents—or even one—I'd kick in your teeth!"

I suggested that he might be a bit more diplomatic.

A volunteer spokesman for the now-unfriendly group shouted, "We'll never go to another one of your pictures!"

The great man answered this threat of boycott with a snarl. "Back to the reform school, you little nose-pickers!"

Fields' chauffeur drove the car slowly out the cemetery gates, where some workmen were pouring concrete into molds for coffin vaults. W. C. said under his breath, "Hope chests!" then added vehemently, "This is my last trip to a cemetery!"

"Aren't you forgetting something?" I asked.

"I'm going to be cremated," retorted Uncle Claude, "even if it causes an explosion, and have my ashes thrown like confetti all around the nineteenth hole of the nearest golf club."

It was midday now, and the California sun made a bath-cabinet of our car. I took off my coat. The perspiring Fields told his chauffeur Stanislaus to draw up in front of the next vacant lot. There my host removed the robe from the floor-refrigerator at our feet and opened the icebox with a delicate flick of his juggler's fingers.

"What would you like, my good nephew? Beer or martinis?"

"Both," I replied.

"A very wise decision," and W. C. beamed upon two pewter mugs that he had conjured from the inside of the box.

We sipped our beer and traveled leisurely toward Hollywood. After a while Uncle Claude said, "Now for the main event."

He put aside the pewter mugs and selected two slender glasses from the refrigerator, which he referred to as Pandora's husband's box. Into one of these glasses he poured a king-size martini from a half-gallon thermos flask. He held his palm over the brim of the glass as he gave it to me, to prevent the spilling of what he called "angel's milk." Then he poured himself a like drink.

"If Falstaff had stuck to martinis," he said, "he'd still be with us. Poor soul!"

Just as we were lifting our glasses the automobile jolted across one of those ditchlike depressions that are supposed to carry off the flash floods of the rainy season. We lost a good deal of our respective drinks, whereupon Fields accused his chauffeur of being a secret agent of the Woman's Christian Temperance Union.

To forestall another occurrence of "sabotage," he ordered Stanislaus to double-park while he refilled our glasses. A police car with two officers in it, one of them a mirthless sergeant, drew alongside.

"You ought to know you can't double-park here," the sergeant called to the chauffeur.

"The hell we can't!" said Fields. He glared at the sergeant and sipped from his glass.

The sergeant at once turned his attention to W. C. "Just what do you think you're doing in there?"

The self-righteous comedian replied, "We are sitting at the crossroads between art and nature, trying to figure out where delirium tremens leaves off and Hollywood begins."

"Oh, you are, eh? Well what's that you got in those glasses?"

"It ain't sassafras tea," Fields said. "Sorry, there's not enough, or I'd invite you to join us. Come to think of it though, I never bribe a peace-enforcement officer. *Auf Wiedersehen.* And twenty-three!"

The sergeant and Fields stared at each other for perhaps twenty seconds. W. C. said, "Get the license number of his car, Stanislaus. Then on our way! We have tarried too long." And we drove off without hindrance.

I could not understand why we were not arrested. "I suppose those cops know you," I suggested.

"They do now," said Mr. Fields, pouring another martini. "I am known to all the blue-bellies of Christendom, including Scotland Yard and the prefects of Paree. Whitey the Weasel, that's one of my monikers. Did I ever tell you of the time I was in Denver and—" He stopped, obviously remembering of a sudden that I had been born in Denver, had spent much of my youth there, and would likely trap him in one of his great big lies.

"Yes?" I said encouragingly. "What happened in Denver, Whitey?"

"Slips my mind," he said uneasily. "Yes! Yes! Slips my

mind. Indeed!" Whenever he was caught lying he would put on a hurt expression, like that of a confidence man nabbed while pawning his grandmother's ear trumpet. He said through his teeth, "It wasn't Denver, you suspicious, narrow-minded bastard! It was Sioux City. Winter of nineteen-six. I remember it so well. Yes indeed! Bitter cold. Wind blowing two hundred knots. And the citizens cowering in their snowed-under domiciles. The Ohio River frozen solid, bank to bank—"

"Don't you mean the Missouri River?" I interrupted slyly. "Or maybe it was the Thames? Or the Seine? Or—"

He broke in savagely, "Sorry I didn't let you go home in the black bus! My little adventure *might* have occurred in Cleveland. But no matter, I was madly in love for a time. Then it wore off. Heard that her father was a crack shot. The lady became a nuisance. But I got rid of her by a clever ruse."

"You broke both her legs?"

"Even more subtle than that. I pinned a note to my dressing-room door at the theater."

"*What* theater?"

"Damn it!" he cried. "Must you cross-examine me? Since when have I ever toyed with historic truth?"

"What did your note say?"

"It said 'Gone for Lunch!' "

"Did she wait for your return?"

"I don't know. I simply don't know. Yes indeed. Because I left for Europe."

W. C. chuckled. "One day I told Jack Barrymore that the foul report about my hating women was a falsehood dreamed up by some jilted spinster. I told Jack that I loved the little nectarines; disliked only the aggressive and possessive types. And he said to me, 'Is there any other kind?' "

As we stopped at a street intersection to wait for the traffic light to turn green one of the funeral limousines came abreast of us. It had in it but one passenger, the always sad-faced impresario of lovely show-girls, Mr. Earl Carroll.

Mr. Carroll bowed gravely to us, and Mr. Fields shouted a profane greeting in return. W. C. then motioned for him to join us. While Carroll was getting out of the black limousine Fields said to me, "Earl was an old program boy. He got shipwrecked once and worked his way back to America as a deckhand. He met several wealthy survivors of the wreck for the first time as he swabbed the decks, and they became patrons of his first show on Broadway. He looks like an unfrocked priest, don't you think?"

"Gentlemen," said Carroll as he got inside to sit between us, "it is always a pleasure to see you."

Fields poured a martini into one of the slender glasses and offered it to Carroll. The impresario examined the glass with much interest but said nothing. I looked more closely at my own glass, to see for the first time that it was decorated with facsimiles of the signatures of famous actresses and actors and bore the label "Earl Carroll's."

Fields showed no embarrassment whatsoever at being the illegal possessor of these restaurant glasses. "Your health, sir," he said to Carroll, "and you look like you could use some of it."

At Carroll's invitation we stopped at his magnificent estate (there were *three* swimming pools on the grounds) in Bel-Air. He served us martinis in beautiful crystal chalices, with the comment, "These glasses were *not* stolen!"

W. C. now wanted to return home, saying he must prepare next Sunday's sermon, but I persuaded him to drop in at Decker's, where I wanted to pick up a deathbed sketch the artist had done of Barrymore. He had brought it to my house the morning after Jack died, then taken it home again to retouch the sketch and put highlights on the brow, the nose, and on a fold beneath the chin.

Decker served drinks in glasses that once had been the property of the Club Ugene, one of our frequent ports of call when other places of its kind were closed for the night.

Fields scrutinized his glass. "My conscience feels easier," he said.

W. C. and I went from the studio to my house, where we talked for half an hour or so in the living room. My friend looked from time to time, with obvious disapproval, at a Decker portrait above the fireplace—an excellent likeness of Sadakichi Hartmann, seated reading a book and smoking a cigar. In the background Decker had painted a group of three almost nude figures hanging upon crosses. The center figure of this scene of crucifixion was John Barrymore, and on either side of him there hung a woman.

EIGHTEEN

Why alight, black crow,
On the fir tree's branch
On this autumn night?
—Sadakichi

I spent eight months on my Barrymore book, and was in no mood to give ear to the outcries of Sadakichi Hartmann. He wrote or telephoned weekly from Banning, to denounce me for not writing *his* biography. He was a much bigger man than Barrymore, he said, and, for that matter, more important to the world of letters than anyone else. Also, he meant to put the evil eye on me and my present work.

Although he behaved like an insulted hobgoblin he still asked for contributions: money, a tent, a stove, clothes, and pastel sticks with which he fashioned landscapes and Greenwich Village scenes prized only by himself.

When I pointed out to him that the war had made anyone of German or Japanese descent most unpopular, in or out of print, the old fellow said, "But I have proof that my mother was a Korean."

"I know," was my reply, "but you can't tell that to the Marines."

Aside from my necessary visits to New York, Chicago, and Philadelphia to interview old friends of Barrymore, I seldom left my house these months except to meet with Jack's former business manager, Henry Hotchener, and his wife Helios. These excellent people had a great store of Barrymore material, hitherto undisclosed to the outside world, diaries and the like.

Of course I would call upon W. C. Fields occasionally, or look in at Decker's, particularly when the artist reported himself in trouble.

One day I found him wearing the icebag on his head and giving himself a shot of insulin. "How do they expect to get it when I haven't got it?" he asked ambiguously.

"Would you be more specific? Get what?"

"Why!" he exclaimed in a tone of indignation. "A nosy son-of-a-bitch from the Revenue Department just left here. Wanted to know why I didn't file an income tax. The nerve of the guy!"

"I've told you several times," I reminded him, "that everyone has to keep track of his income and pay the tax."

"But I'm an artist!" he said.

"That in itself is a criminal offense in the eyes of most people. You'd better do something about the tax."

"The pirate's chest is empty," he said. "And besides, Bill Fields told me to disregard the whole thing."

"I hardly think Uncle Claude is a good judge of these matters. The government made him pay through the nose. He's lucky to stay out of the cooler."

How Decker finally managed the tax problem he never would say. If asked about it he would wink or smile mysteriously.

On another occasion of an appeal for help he said he really was in trouble this time. "I'm a bigamist!" He groaned.

"That so?" I asked. "Suppose you brief me?"

"My first wife and daughter are on the scene, and you've simply got to help me."

"I thought you were divorced from your first wife?"

"I'd forgot all about Helen when I married Phyllis," he said. "It slipped my mind."

My painter friend had an interesting though untenable theory that if he forgot an untoward happening in his personal history everyone else was bound to forget it. The upswing of his fame and fortune, as so often happens to men of more talent than horse sense, had invited the attention of income-tax investigators and of lawyers who specialize in pointing up the mistakes of groggy lovers.

Decker's first wife and daughter had recently read in the New York newspapers that the artist was prospering in California. Mrs. Decker had not seen, or heard from, her mercurial husband for perhaps fifteen or sixteen years. Daughter Gloria suggested they go West to congratulate the genius on his triumphs.

"I remember something from my newspaper experience," I remarked to Decker. "It has to do with a statute called the Enoch Arden law. You'll have to let an attorney advise you on this; but I think that if you can prove your wife disappeared for several years, and you believed her dead, you may get out of this jam."

"I'll see a mouthpiece at once," said Decker. "I wish I were a Moslem."

The artist filed suit for divorce from Helen Decker, saying that she had left him in 1928 and that he had not set eyes upon her since the summer of 1929. The case was heard before Judge Jess E. Stephens in Superior Court in July 1943. Decker testified that he had made every reasonable effort to learn of his wife's whereabouts, failed in this, presumed she was dead, then married a second time.

"Were these efforts made before or after you had arrived as an artist?" the judge asked.

"An artist," Decker replied, "never arrives until he is dead."

The judge granted a decree of divorce. He said from the bench, "It might constitute cruel and unusual punishment to make a man go through life with two wives."

On his way out of the courtroom Decker was greeted by an admirer. "I dreamed of you last night," she twittered.

"Do I owe you anything?" asked Decker.

Still another woman asked what he did to keep his hair in its splendid condition of growth and sheen. "Soap, madam," he said. "Plain laundry soap, and no water."

The woman seemed incredulous and said as much, but Decker had spoken the truth. He had very dark red hair, with not a thread of gray in it, and never washed it; instead he would dampen a bar of common laundry soap and smear it on his hair and into his scalp each morning. This sort of treatment, I was told, would cause most persons to go bald in a matter of weeks.

Few persons care, nor should they, to hear about an author's problems in the writing of his book. Nor would I mention my own difficulties in respect to the Barrymore book did I not wish to convey to some faltering pilgrim the importance of holding on in a time of distress.

I had no conscious intention of writing about John Barrymore when he was still alive; and when I undertook to do his life it was as a memorial to a great friend, with little thought of the book's critical acceptance or of my own financial betterment. I had experienced the mere making of much money, and the spending of it. As to the literary value of my work, I needed no pundit to remind me that it did not measure up to that of Washington Irving. I desired to live and to let live, and I had the compulsion to write, no matter how remiss I may have been in both respects. That has been my passion always in this glad but seldom understood way of life.

The least of the troubles that began to close in upon me was the recommendation that I undergo surgery for appendicitis. I decided against the operation and kept right on with my book. Nor did I ever part with my appendix. Then a severe heart attack—in fact, three of them, in jolting succession—threatened to strike me out; but I went back to my desk each time. Several other problems beset me from all sides, as often happens when we are most vulnerable.

I kept up a show of courage, for I am a stubborn man; but there were times when I secretly felt like picking up my marbles and going to the lonely hills, as my father had done long ago. I am ashamed to admit it, but I was about to become a quitter.

There were eleven commandments, I think, instead of ten; and Moses somehow lost the eleventh one during his descent from Sinai: "Thou shalt not quit."

Just as I was putting on smoked glasses, as it were, to see my own eclipse, a letter arrived from Robert Edmond Jones, a stranger to me but whose creative work I had long admired. Mr. Jones had been the foremost stage-set designer of the golden age of the American theater. He had created the scenic backgrounds for Barrymore's *Hamlet* and for two other plays in which genius flowered.

Mr. Jones's letter had in it a paragraph that persuaded me to take off my smoked glasses for all time:

> Dr. Jung (the one who isn't Freud, you know) told me once that whenever anything really creative is in hand, all the powers of Hell rise up to say that it shall not be brought about—and one may expect illness, accidents, all kinds of negative happenings, until the real thing comes to pass, seemingly of itself.

An unexpected right word comes like a knocking at the door in the night of one's near despair!

There would be other days and other books for me; and Decker would paint more pictures, some good, and some not so good, but never ordinary ones; Sadakichi stayed on at the reservation for many months; and Uncle Claude made what was to be his last motion-picture, *The Bank Dick*.

"The old bastard is getting meaner every day," La Cava said.

Fields wrote to me frequently, and I to him; and each morning after reading the newspapers he telephoned, to lambaste almost everything that wartime Washington was doing or not doing. I shook in my shoes whenever Uncle Claude got on his soapbox, and felt sure that we would go to prison, were someone to listen in on his tirades. London's Hyde Park never saw or heard his like.

Among the things he said were: "Benedict Arnold has risen from the tomb to sell us out again." And, "So-and-so has missed everything but his father's wedding."

One day Decker, LaCava, and I called at the comedian's house to find him studying a large map in which he stuck varicolored pins from day to day, to show the movements of the belligerents.

Fields regarded himself as a military as well as a naval authority, and seldom approved the tactics of anyone except Admiral Halsey and Generals MacArthur and Patton. Samples of his adverse criticism of the high brass on both sides of the conflict were: "Admiral Darlan couldn't even row a canoe at Vassar!" "General Montgomery can't find his backside with both hands!" "Von Runstedt is the biggest horse's buttock since the wooden one of ancient Troy!"

Decker, after inspecting Uncle Claude's war map, asked him why one of the many red pins—used by W. C. to indicate Hitler's progress by land or by sea—was placed in Boise, Idaho. Fields interpreted this query as a deliberate slur on his integrity as a war correspondent.

"It's a German submarine base!" our host snarled. "And just for your uncalled-for remark, I'm cutting you out of my will."

Apropos of nothing, or so it seemed to us, he announced that he also was leaving his brother Walter out of the will. He alleged in passing that Walter once had been given a contract by the government to install ten miles of telegraph poles in Alaska.

"How did he make out?" LaCava inquired.

"Nary a pole did he plant in the frozen tundra," replied Uncle Claude. "Blew an easy fortune. Said his hands were too cold."

As the months passed Hartmann did not telephone frequently, but occasionally wrote me about his troubles. He expected to be interned any day now, notwithstanding the fact that he had become a citizen of the United States in 1884, and would be persecuted, he felt, simply because he had been born in Japan.

"Confucius said," he pointed out, "that the human soul can go everywhere. The federal investigators manage to go still further. They find out everything, and they will bother everybody I know with, 'What shall we do with this man Hartmann?' "

He wrote that his health was so "atrocious" that he did not care much what might happen, but thought it a disgrace to drive an old invalid poet from place to place, homeless, as Dante had been. "I am afraid of the officials in small towns," he said. "So, after all, I'd better go to Los Angeles to see a lawyer and get a travel permit."

In another letter he said, "The real Sadakichi Hartmann you once knew died in 1940, soon after the sabotage train wreck near Akron, which gave Decker, Barrymore, and you so much cause for laughter. What is left is merely an extension that will withdraw, evaporate. I am not as lucky as Christ, who died for the second time forty days after the Crucifixion."

He meant to go to New York, where the Japanese were not so conspicuously hounded as in California. He would die soon, he predicted, and he regarded life as not worth living.

"Send him some money quick!" Decker said. "Or he'll move in here, and we'll all go to prison."

Sadakichi's friend Ben Marx sent me some money to forward to Hartmann and suggested that other friends contribute to the old poet's contemplated journey East. I sent this money, together with my own check, to Hartmann, who promptly denounced Marx for not having mailed the cash directly to him. Hartmann referred to the donations as the "Liverwurst Drive," and got ready to leave California.

One evening late in January of 1944 Sadakichi left the reservation to get a drink at a Banning bar. As he was crossing the road an automobile almost ran him down.

Sadakichi denounced the driver of the car, then changed his tune to ask, "Where are you going?"

"Just along the highway."

"All life is a highway," Hartmann said. "And I want to go with you."

He got into the car and, as had happened before, eventually arrived at Decker's studio. John called off the party he was preparing in honor of his wife's birthday; in self-defense he disregarded his diabetes and began to drink heavily.

It so happened that I was out of the city and did not return home until early the next day. It was a very cold day for California. A strong wind drove the rain against one's face with the sting of a wet whip. I found a sheaf of telephone messages on my desk, several of them from Decker, who asked that I come to the studio at the first opportunity.

I found the artist in a state of near-collapse in the Valentino chair. He had on an elegant maroon dressing gown and was looking fixedly, and silently, at Sadakichi. Decker's dachshund Gus also was watching Sadakichi, who sat across the room on a couch.

The old intruder was wearing the camel's-hair overcoat Decker had given him some four years before. All the buttons were off, and a large safety pin was fastened to it, like a policeman's badge. His sparse beard had been unshaven for some days.

Hartmann's jaws were working up and down on a ham sandwich. While sitting there eating and spouting excerpts from his own poems, he allowed the sandwich to dangle for a moment from his long fingers. In a flash the dachshund seized the meat and darted away. Sadakichi left off muttering his verses to curse the dog in German.

I asked Decker if he needed a doctor. The staring artist shook his head. He roused from his trancelike state to go slowly to his easel, near which an unstrung archer's bow stood on end. "I meant to get an arrow," he said, picking up the bow, "and fix this weapon for just such an occasion as this." He turned to Sadakichi. "But what good would it do? I'd shoot at you and probably miss!"

"Thank you very much," Sadakichi replied. Then he predicted that he had less than a year to live, that W. C. Fields would go in two years, Decker in three; and he advised me to have all my affairs straightened out before I shuffled off in four.

"If I finance your trip East," I said, "would you give me ten more years?"

He thought this over. "I'll even make it twelve."

"This is blackmail," I said, "but it's a deal."

Decker received a letter from Sadakichi, written at Banning under the date of January 30, 1944. It contained the critical verdict the artist had awaited for many years. It read in part:

> What I have to offer at the moment is not so much an estimate but a few words from a veteran critic to a full-fledged artist. I was amazed (that is the right word) at the enormity of the output; I would say forty or fifty canvases, and all on par, so far away and beyond the shystermagoria of your "Old Masters," and done in a remarkably short span of time.
>
> What has suddenly come over and into you? Your sickness, isolation, loneliness, abstention from drinking? The departure of Barrymore must have something to do with this transformation. What I admire first of all is the vigorous groping for a new technique—fluency of expression and a devil-may-care nonchalance toward the medium. What I like best is the row of houses in the ghost town; the distortion and strange combination of anatomical structures; and what you call "clowns," those

gruesome bastard derelicts that I would not like to meet in life. . . . They are so uncouth that they are the great and uncanny inventions of a superbly weird imagination.

Yes, John Decker, you are a great painter—if you can keep it up.

Decker prized this letter more than he did the honors that had come to him. He never heard again from the strange old man who had seemed in our eyes a weirdly fashioned person of brilliant mind and knavish impulses— but ever a disciple of beauty and of integrity in his own world of art and of the artist.

That November we received word that Sadakichi Hartmann had died at the home of one of his daughters, Mrs. Dorothea Gilliland, in St. Petersburg, Florida.

NINETEEN

Like mist on the leas,
Fall gently, O rain of spring.
        —Sadakichi

One Sunday in September of 1944 Dave Chasen and Ben Smith of Wall Street invited Fields, Decker, and me to go to the horse races in Tijuana. Decker couldn't make it because he was getting ready to move, with the financial backing of Errol Flynn, to a larger studio. Fields said he would go in his own car and meet us at the border.

Chasen, Smith, and I started out early in the day and toward noon arrived at the customs station sixteen miles below San Diego. Uncle Claude already was on the scene as we drove up, and we got ready to cross over to Lower California. W. C. said that he preferred to continue the journey in his own car, since we had nothing to drink in ours and the country abounded in venomous snakes on the lookout for visiting Americans.

An official explained that we must declare any currency

we might severally possess and exchange it for an equivalent amount in two-dollar bills. This regulation had been designed to forestall the importation into Mexico of American banknotes of assorted denomination, and the consequent danger of enemy agents collecting, then forwarding this stabilized money abroad. Any bulky shipment from Mexico of two-dollar bills could be easily detected by the authorities.

"If you think I'm going to change my dough into two-dollar bills," W. C. announced, "you'd better consult an alienist!"

The customs official patiently went over the situation once again with tourist Fields. "It's a rule," he said, "and everyone must obey it."

Uncle Claude put the evil eye upon his latest enemy. "I make my own rules! Always have. Always will."

"If you please!" the government man said. "You're holding up traffic."

"And you're trying to hold me up!" retorted Fields. "Two-dollar bills are a jinx. One side, laddie buck! Avast!"

I find myself quite at sea in trying to explain the effrontery of this man. Time and again he would bluster his way out of situations that would have meant jail for less hardy persons. All I can say is that this time the customs man permitted W. C. to keep his money intact; the rest of us accepted the exchange without protest.

As Fields crossed the border in his car he leaned out to display his bankroll. "Take a good look at this poke!" he shouted. "Three grand! And I earned it with the sweat of my brow and of other hidden parts of the body."

We had a fine time of it that Sunday at the racetrack, although Uncle Claude complained that the course ran uphill part of the way. He wagered on each race, not heavily, to be sure; bought Mexican food and beer for the party, and would accept no two-dollar banknotes offered in change for the tens or twenties he boldly flourished while paying the check.

W. C. seemed tired but reasonably happy as we got ready to leave Tijuana, and thanked a turf official for not having been "too crooked" in conducting the races.

Ben Smith asked that we stop over in San Diego on our way home to see a good friend, Captain William A. Maguire of the United States Navy. Captain Maguire, a Roman Catholic priest, was acclaimed a war hero for his services while chaplain of the Pacific Fleet.

Mr. Smith inquired if I would do him a personal favor, and I said yes. Would I send Captain Maguire a check for a thousand dollars of Mr. Smith's money and pretend that it was I who gave it?

Although Smith is a man of many good deeds, he has a strong desire that no one shall know anything about them. He also is a superb salesman, and that day he had nearly convinced me to pose as a philanthropist when W. C. intervened. Fields' ears were as sharp as a piano tuner's, and he had overheard what Ben Smith had been saying to me.

"Don't you give that dominie one farthing in your own name," W. C. protested. "If you do, you'll find yourself on a sucker list forevermore."

The good Father eventually received the thousand dollars; lighted a candle and said a prayer for Ben Smith; and wrote me that he had used the gift as a down payment on a pipe-organ for his church in San Diego.

Decker's new studio was just south of Sunset Strip on Alta Loma Drive, a hundred feet or less back of Hollywood's finest night club, the Mocambo. This studio had been built by the artist and color expert, Dr. Hilaire Hiler, and for a time had been occupied by him. It had a large main room, with long skylights and enough wall space to accommodate pictures for purposes of commercial exhibition.

Errol Flynn just recently had entered a partnership of sorts with Decker, and they went downtown to purchase furniture and drapes for the studio. While shopping they came upon a lifelike manikin at one of the wholesale establishments, which they purchased at a good price.

Decker named the nude figure Mona and propped it up in a sitting position against the rear cushions of Flynn's convertible. As they drove along the highways their nude model understandably attracted a good deal of attention. Flynn was widely known as a ladies' man, and when the supposed quite naked blonde was seen riding in his automobile the onlookers may well have assumed that he was pressing his luck.

Mona became an important part of the scene at the new studio. Indeed, she was the cause of a fistfight between two gentlemen who grew overzealous about having the next dance with her. Life at the Alta Loma studio was of a more bustling nature than at Bundy Drive; but to me, and to the others who had looked upon the old cottage as an artistic Alamo, the more modern quarters did not allow us to shut out Hollywood's banalities, her trumped-up glories, her shallow deeds.

Decker, however, seemed to enjoy his new surroundings. He prospered, but of course did not hold onto his money. He gave a succession of one-man shows, upped his prices, made a new garden, and placed the pirate's chest in an alcove off his art library.

The first picture Decker painted at the Alta Loma studio was a backyard scene of the Mocambo at night. Outside the club, in the glow cast from the rear windows, stood the ugly trash boxes and garbage cans among the weeds; and above the backyard, on the other side of the window, sat the swank merrymakers in evening dress. Decker called this picture "Pigs in Clover."

Charles Morrison, proprietor of the night club, was invited in to see the picture. He took no offense, and from that time on befriended Decker, bought several pictures, and would not allow him to pay for meals or drinks at the club. Decker, of course, stood his own tips; but if out of pocket money, as he usually was, would borrow a five or a ten from a companion and with a flourish hand it to the waiter or the doorman.

Some time after Decker and Flynn acquired Mona there was a free-for-all at the studio. This was another reminder that the Bundy Drive days forever were gone. Not within my memory had anyone exchanged punches at the old place. True, a sculptor had flung his wife part way into the open fireplace while the coals were hot, but merely to illustrate the way he had acted toward her in the days before a psychoanalyst had cured him of his bursts of temper.

At Bundy Drive sarcasms often had been exchanged, and a bit of drinking done; but no damage had been dealt out, except to the furniture or the eardrums of neighbors. Offensive strangers had seldom intruded; if they did, they conformed to the spirit of the scene or soon found themselves outside.

Now there were new faces to be seen. The world moved in on the artist, on his health, and, in certain respects, on his work at the easel.

And good friends had died, or were dying.

One night even Mona could no longer stand the pace. An actor knocked down the son of a famous actress. Someone got a fractured skull. The guests chose sides, and the battle was joined. Mona was shattered.

The police came while Decker was sadly trying to put Mona together again. "Who hit who?" a policeman asked.

"How in hell would I know?" said the artist. "I was busy trying to protect Mona."

"Who's Mona?"

"You wouldn't understand," Decker said. "I know nothing."

Some months after the Tijuana journey I stopped in at Jack Dempsey's to ask that he allow John Decker to paint his portrait.

Dempsey and I had been close friends ever since his young manhood in Colorado, where both of us had been born. I wanted very much to own a portrait of him, not as the great athlete whom I had seen fight his way up from poverty and obscurity to the heavyweight championship, but as a person of strong character, a quality that had enabled him to survive blows much more damaging than anyone's fists can give a man.

I saw him then as I see him now: a forthright man, strong in all ways, tempered though not mellowed by time; a man whose early environment might well have sent anyone of lesser moral endurance on the wrong road. Other artists might paint a good likeness of Dempsey, and some of them have done so; but Decker, I felt certain, would see the man himself instead of his mere semblance or his reputation.

Dempsey readily agreed to sit for his portrait. Then he said with some concern, "I've noticed lately that Bill Fields has been keeping his bedroom lights on all night. Is he all right?"

Dempsey was living on Los Feliz Boulevard, not far down the hill from Fields' house. The two men were very good friends, but somehow were reluctant to call on each other. If I were to risk an opinion on this seeming social indifference of the two neighbors, and not be asked to prove my point, I would say that both men actually were shy persons. This interpretation, I am well aware, may be set down as so much rubbish by the tens of thousands who have seen the dark and scowling captain of the boxers charge like a killer in the prize ring and beat his opponents to the canvas-covered boards; and it may also be discounted by those who have seen the blustering, flamboyant comedian play his public roles or in private shout his evasive answers to officers of the law. Nevertheless I think there is a shyness hidden within the selves of many successful men, almost a sense of timidity, a thing that a public idol must never reveal or admit even to himself.

Strangely enough, whenever I visited one or the other of these men, he would ask how his neighbor was faring and promise to make a call, but never did. I think each was reluctant to intrude upon the other's privacy.

"Let's look in on W. C. right now," I suggested to Dempsey.

"You go ahead," he replied. "I may drop in on him tomorrow."

"All right." Then I said mischievously, "I guess you're still upset about what happened last night, eh?"

My sturdy friend did not relish this remark. "I hope it won't get in the newspapers."

Early that same morning the governess of Dempsey's two young daughters had roused him from sleep with the cry, "Quick, Mr. Dempsey! Something shameful has happened! The swimming pool!"

The ex-champion didn't wait for a long count, as at the time he had knocked down Gene Tunney in Chicago. He ran downstairs and out of the house. In the moonlight he saw someone splashing about, quite naked, in the swimming pool.

"Hey! What do you think you're doing there?" Dempsey shouted. "Get out, and get your clothes on! But quick!"

The swimmer replied matter-of-factly, "Why don't you let me alone? I'm enjoying myself and hurting no one."

"For the last time," Dempsey warned, "I'm telling you to get out. Or I'm coming in after you."

"Aw, go to hell!" the man said, floating down to the shallow end.

At this Dempsey jumped into the pool, stood chest deep in the water, and cuffed the intruder's ears. The ex-champion of the world took a suitable stance on the shallow bottom of the pool, then lifted the fellow from the water and prepared to hurl him ashore. But a feeling of utmost dismay stayed Dempsey's purpose.

"Good lord!" Dempsey told me. "What will people say if they find out I hit a midget!"

"They'll think you're trying to come back," I said. "By easy stages, of course."

After I left Dempsey I put in an appearance at Fields' house, only to learn that he had gone to the polls. It was an election day, and he had left word that he was voting against everybody.

I awaited his return. As he got out of his car I could not help observing that his legs were enfeebled, the ankles swollen, as if from dropsy. I half carried him upstairs to his office. He protested that I was maliciously trying to show him up as a helpless invalid and refused to go to bed, saying it was the most unsafe place in the world, that people constantly were dying in bed—or, worse still, being born there.

"I'm going to move out of this house," he said later.

"Where to?"

"I neither know nor care."

I offered to make a place for him in my own home. For

once he did not look at me with a suspicious, belligerent eye. He smiled. "Thanks," he said, as though he really meant it, and added, "I'm remembering you in my will. Meanwhile, my kindly sir, pour yourself a little token of my esteem."

"I'd prefer a glass of milk if you don't mind—that is, if you have any in the house."

"Mind!" he cried out. "Have you no sense of decency? Milk!"

"Tell me," I asked, "when did you last have a drink of milk?"

"An hour before I left my dear mother!" he said. "Now go!"

Soon after this Uncle Claude put into storage his big desk, the pool table, the rowing machine, his several bars, the sets of Dickens and Mark Twain, and his numerous gadgets. He entered a sanitarium at Las Encinas, near Pasadena, and took up residence in a small bungalow on the grounds, a stuccoed building with a walled-in patio. There he waited each day in a rocking chair for the coming of the Man in the Bright Nightgown.

He spent much of the time, especially at night, in writing a codicil to his will and deciding what remembrances he would leave to his friends. The provisions of this handwritten document afterward were ruled out in probate court or were long delayed in execution.

I talked to W. C. by telephone almost every day and called him long distance when I was in the East on business. I would go the thirty miles between my home and the sanitarium to visit him as often as I could manage to do so during the year and a half he lived on at the rest home. In his last months he openly established a bar in his bedroom. The doctors had come to agree that he surely would die at once were he to quit drinking.

"And they could have saved their breath," he snorted. "It's like warning a madam to quit knocking sex."

I paid him a visit a few days before Christmas of 1946. He had been confined to his bed for three weeks or so. I got up enough courage to ask him if he actually disliked the holiday or if it was merely a stubborn pretense.

"Well," he replied, as best I can remember his words, "it was this way: I believed in Christmas until I was eight years old. I had saved up some money carrying ice in Philadelphia. I was going to buy my mother a copper-bottom clothes boiler for Christmas. I kept the money hidden in a brown crock in the coalbin. My father found the crock. He did exactly what I would have done in his place. He stole the money. And ever since then I've remembered nobody on Christmas, and I want nobody to remember me either. Is that clear?"

The day before Christmas I telephoned the Fields bungalow to arrange to visit him the next afternoon. Someone, a woman whose voice I did not recognize, informed me that Mr. Fields could not answer the telephone and that he would receive no visitors until after the first of the year. The polite but ambiguous replies to my other questions caused me some concern.

Nor could I obtain further information when I telephoned the sanitarium Christmas morning. I decided to go out there as soon as I completed the holiday calls on my children and their respective families.

I remember it as a gray morning, cold and rainy, very cold and very gray. I did not know this at the time, but two of Fields' close friends, Dave Chasen and Billy Grady, already were at Las Encinas. They had taken with them some delicacies and a case of whisky for W. C. To him whisky was not merely a delicacy but a necessity.

Just as Chasen and Grady were about to go through the patio gateway they saw two men carrying out a long basket, and in it lay Uncle Claude's body. The rain of the gray Christmas, a day he always had pretended to abhor, beat down upon the men and upon the basket.

It was about noon when someone at Las Encinas managed to learn where I was and telephoned me at my son Will's house. There was now no need for me to make the journey to Las Encinas.

I was told that, just before W. C. Fields died (he had been in a coma for several hours) he opened his eyes, then winked.

TWENTY

Calm joyous days cannot be wooed
Unless our conscience is at peace.
                    —Sadakichi

About eleven months before Fields winked at the Man in the Bright Nightgown I went to New York to work on the galley proofs of a book. Among the messages at the publisher's office was a note to call Mrs. Sadakichi Hartmann.

The first wife of the late Sadakichi, Betty Walsh Hartmann, had a pleasing voice over the telephone. Had she not mentioned her seventy-eighth birthday, and had I not known something of her story, I might have thought her a much younger woman, perhaps a singer or an actress. She gave me her address, a walk-up apartment on the fourth floor of a flat in the East Eighties, near the river.

It was a windy afternoon in January when I went uptown to see her. Gray dunes of neglected snow from a storm some weeks earlier stood in the gutters of the side streets—seasonal reminders that New York is among the world's most slovenly housekeepers. In summer her streets are littered and dirty. In winter she wears her grimy snow as an aging harlot does a frowzy ermine wrap left over from more affluent times.

The house was an old one, of the trite sameness of plan that tenement builders favored just before the financial panic of 1893. I pressed the buzzer in the downstairs vestibule but received no response. From the nearest drugstore I telephoned Mrs. Hartmann that her communication system was out of order. She said she would come downstairs to let me in. Mindful of her age, I asked that she give me a few minutes to return to the house, and then, if the release latch did not function, come down the stairs to unlock the door.

As I waited for the lock to click I heard the horns of the river boats, a chorus that always made me think of slaves mourning for old Massa. Random thoughts came to mind. I remembered other cold gray afternoons when, as a young newspaper reporter in the Big Town, I had fancied that I would amount to something one day. All I had to do, or so I had believed long ago, was to keep on knocking at doors. The right one would open, surely, if I persisted, and my knuckles did not fail me.

I found myself smiling, as though politely tolerant of a chance meeting with someone I once had known quite well but now had almost forgotten; someone who had come out of the past to chat with me for just a moment, show me some fragments of a remote yesterday, and then disappear into the wintry mist of time. That other person had been quite naïve, I thought, and dream-struck, and had knocked at many doors. . . .

I heard a creaking of stairs, and the door was opened by an elderly woman in a gray dress, the style of which I cannot name, but which seemed to belong, as did its wearer, to a time when well-groomed ladies arrived in horse-drawn carriages at much nobler doors than this one.

Mrs. Hartmann studied me with fine blue eyes set wide apart. She was rather tall, straight and strong, and my first impression was that in her young years she probably had been quite handsome, if not beautiful.

We climbed three flights of vaguely seen stairs and entered a long, narrow apartment. The front room overlooked the street, where boys were playing stick-and-ball. The deep, sad, contrapuntal horns of the river boats mingled with the shouts and laughter of the children.

The living room contained, besides a few pieces of heavy furniture, a medley of Victorian and Oriental bric-a-brac. On the mantelpiece of the false fireplace stood a silver-framed photograph of Sadakichi in his early thirties. The profile view showed his long jaw, his then black heap of hair, and one fawn-like ear. He wore a small mustache, close-cropped, and the one eye that could be seen in the photograph had a quizzical expression, touched with some special sort of pain and hunger.

Mrs. Hartmann frequently glanced up at this photograph as she sat opposite me in an old-fashioned, velvet-tufted chair. Beside her, on a table of heavy oak, rested a small Buddhist shrine of brass. A kerosene-fueled stove in front of the false fireplace gave off fumes that reminded me of the smell of Sadakichi's pipe.

Mrs. Hartmann showed me a photostatic copy of her marriage certificate. From it I learned that she had been the daughter of a British Army officer, and had been born in Bermuda. Mrs. Hartmann said that she had met Sadakichi soon after his attempt at suicide. I asked her if the episode of the slashed wrist had not been a warning for her to expect other weird actions on the part of the man she would marry.

She replied calmly, "I don't think women ever take warning when they are in love."

I sought to be discreet in questioning this obviously well-bred, intelligent person. But there had been several matters in respect to Sadakichi's character and actions I had been unable to clarify in my own mind. Perhaps she could explain some of them. Why, for example, were many women attracted to Sadakichi? He himself had egotistically asserted that these women had pampered him, overlooked his "few" faults, and even felt honored by his abuse.

"My husband," she said quite frankly and with no show of rancor, "was entirely self-centered, forgetful, and inattentive. However, he loved children very much, and they loved him. I stayed in the background while he play-acted as the King of Bohemia. I did not revile him when he had a child by another woman. Screams do not remedy a great wrong. He left home one day, on the pretext of getting his health back, and went to California. Not only did he desert me and our five children, but he neglected to write."

"But you continued to love him?"

"I still love him. He was three parts genius and one part devil. I was in love with all four parts. You would have to be a woman to understand that."

"But the other women in his life?" I asked. "Did they love

all four parts of his composite, as you have put it? His mind? Or his physical charms—if that is the right word? What made the New England poetess love him to such a self-ruinous extreme?"

She replied with an air of finality, "He was capable."

Mrs. Hartmann did not elaborate upon this statement. Nor did I think it wise to insist that she do so. Because of her earnestness, I felt that she, as well as the other women who had been devoted to Sadakichi, had somehow found in him, or else in their own concepts of him, the physical and mental potency more commonly come upon in story books than in life.

Mrs. Hartmann had saved pages of manuscript written by her husband during their time together. She asked if she might read one of these pages to me. Only a man of superior intelligence, she said, could have written as Sadakichi did, as early as 1895:

In the life of the Puritans all worship of the beautiful was wanting. All intellectual Americans are Puritans. The hand of God and the claw of the devil are still upon us. The artist as well as the public bears the troubled conscience of sinners. The slightest trespass may scandalize the taste of the drawing room and forfeit success. Puritanism still deals out banishment, confiscation, punishment to unfettered, poetic souls.

The nude has no place in the home, but is relegated to the barroom for the gratification of lewd sensations. It is the insincere modesty of the fig leaf, the hypocrisy of a dyspeptic generation of pedants. We remain a gray race, our passions cold, and a petty, pallid taste pervades our world of arts and letters.

As I took leave of Mrs. Hartmann, I could not help thinking of several other women I had known, women who not only had been in love with the men who flagrantly neglected them but, when their men died, stayed in love with their ghosts. I do not pretend to understand such matters, but would warn any lovesick fellow who woos a widow to make sure, first, he is not competing with a ghost. He is bound to lose.

I returned to California that spring of 1946 to find that my friend Decker had gone to San Francisco with Errol Flynn and the latter's physician, Dr. Frank G. Nolan, for the opening of the artist's one-man show. Sixty-four of his paintings were to be exhibited at the DeYoung Museum. Decker, I was told, was ignoring his diabetes, and was suffering from a chronic stomach ailment. Flynn's doctor watched over the artist and revived him whenever he took to the bottle.

This one-man show increased Decker's prestige. He explained to the Golden Gate art critics that he was trying in his work "to hit the dividing line between the tightness of the ancients and the looseness of the moderns—the borderline between sanity and insanity."

While walking around San Francisco, Decker and Dr. Nolan chanced to pass an antique shop in the window of which a somewhat large oil painting was displayed.

"Look, Frank!" Decker exclaimed. "It's a Modigliani. A genuine one. I'm sure of it. I once knew the man, and I know his work."

They went inside the shop, and Decker shrewdly said to

the proprietor, "What are you asking, if anything, for that copy of a Modigliani in the window?"

"Six hundred dollars. It's a very good copy."

Decker had the shopkeeper take the picture from its place, examined it, then shook his head. "It's a fair copy," he said, "but I wouldn't give more than two hundred for it; and even that's highway robbery." To Dr. Nolan he whispered, "This is a gem."

The shopkeeper and Decker argued back and forth, and finally the artist paid four hundred dollars for the picture. Decker took it with him to his hotel, but not immediately to his suite. He propped the Modigliani against the counter of the Western Union branch office in the lobby and composed the following telegram to Thomas Mitchell:

> My dear Tom: I have spotted an authentic Modigliani, a real beauty, one of his best. Owner does not know its value, and I think you can get it for two thousand dollars if you act quickly.

Mitchell's private art collection was a notable one, and Decker had been one of his several agents, as when Mitchell acquired a small painting by Rembrandt of the head of Our Lord.

The actor telephoned from Beverly Hills, then wired a money order. Decker boasted to everyone except Mitchell about his quick profit of sixteen hundred dollars. Mitchell had no cause for complaint. Some years later he resold the Modigliani for fifteen thousand dollars!

That June, Dr. Nolan and Miss Patsy Parker were married in Decker's studio. Almost all of the Hollywood elite were there. The doctor had been a commander in the United States Navy and had been decorated for heroism in the Pacific theater of war. He and his pretty wife went to live in Decker's old studio on Bundy Drive.

When Decker had moved to his new studio his lease on the old one had another year to go. But he had neglected to notify his landlady, Miss Ellen Brooks, and also had overlooked paying the rent as it had come due each month. Nor had he bothered to reply to her letters. Besides, he had permitted several of his friends, his barber, his butcher, his liquor dealer, to live there free from time to time, until they could find homes elsewhere during the housing shortage caused by the war.

Miss Brooks, a former motion-picture actress, came West to find out what was happening to her house. She sold the property to Dr. Nolan, forgave the amount of rent due her, and even forgave Decker. Almost everyone did.

That summer Errol Flynn (who had some time before been secretly married to Nora Eddington) bought a yacht, his second one, the auxiliary schooner *Zaca,* and invited Decker to go on a coastwise cruise. Among the sixteen other guests were Flynn's scholarly father, Dr. Theodore Thompson-Flynn, a zoologist, and dean of the school of science at Queens College in Belfast, Ireland; and Professor Carl L. Hubbs, noted ichthyologist of the Scripps Institute of Oceanography at La Jolla, California. The voyage was to be a scientific expedition, to collect marine specimens, as well as a pleasure cruise.

There was no word from the sea-faring scientists until the

yacht hove-to off Acapulco. Then we heard that Decker had mutinied against Mrs. Flynn. The next thing we knew, he had flown home with several paintings he had made of Mexican scenes and a mental picture of Mrs. Flynn that he proceeded to paint in profane words.

"Women, men, and yachts," he said, "don't mix."

Decker exhibited his Mexican pictures in January of 1947. Critical opinion was mixed. The pictures had been painted on small boards for the most part, because the artist had not wished to carry with him any bulky materials. The colors, some critics believed, were too hot and had been assembled with less care and skill than the artist had shown in his best work at Bundy Drive.

Decker would do several splendid pictures in the months to come, but now he seemed more indifferent than ever to his ill health, and wasted much time in nightly visits to the Sunset Strip restaurants and clubs.

One evening, when Decker was quite drunk at the Mocambo, Jack Dempsey came in with a pretty young woman, the daughter of one of his old friends. Dempsey is not a drinking man. He will take an occasional highball; but until he was forty years old had seldom tasted more than a glass of beer.

Decker happened to say something akin to the "evasive answer" of the late W. C. Fields, and Dempsey turned away. I knew then that I never would have the portrait of Jack I had wanted Decker to paint.

In May of 1947 I went to New York to work on my book *Beau James*, the life-story of James J. Walker, former Mayor of the City of New York. While there I suffered another heart seizure, a severe one, but insisted upon returning to California.

I do not remember too clearly the days I lay in the Pullman bed, except that no nurse could be obtained because of the postwar shortage, and that a wonderful porter, an old man who had known Jimmy Walker and looked after his wants on several transcontinental journeys, attended me faithfully.

I arrived home and went to bed, and was told that John Decker had gone to the hospital. He was to undergo, for the second time within a week, surgical treatment of a stomach that no longer could take the kind of punishment he had given it.

He made but one telephone call from the hospital. He called my house, but I could not answer the telephone. Nor could I go now to the side of my gifted friend.

Have they drunk, laughed, and sung in vain?
Do grove and grange no longer yield
The Idyls of Theocritus?
                                    —Sadakichi

Many tales were told of John Decker's last days, of how he painted the town instead of the plywood boards stacked against his easel. When everyone else had left the clubs or the cafés the artist would go home at daybreak, to put an icebag on his head and recite excerpts from *Cyrano de Bergerac* into the microphone of a voice-recording machine.

"To sing, to laugh, to dream, to walk in my own way, and be alone . . ."

There was one man who had vitality enough to stay up with Decker night after night, Philip Paval. This Danish artist had studied painting and sculpture but was best known for his work with silver and gold.

Paval watched Decker paint his last works, among them an unfinished portrait of Dave Chasen's wife Maude, and one of Gladys Glad, at this time the wife of Mark Hellinger.

"John was feeling pretty bad," Paval said. "Hellinger had asked him to get the portrait done in time for his wife's birthday. I think he had been paid for it a long time ago, and at last got around to doing it. Tremendous big work, beautiful picture."

"Gladys Glad," I said, "was the last of Flo Ziegfeld's breathtakers."

"Well, anyway," Paval went on, "I brought my car over to Alta Loma, and I put the picture on top of the car, and we drove to Hellinger's. We arrived about one-thirty in the afternoon. Gladys said we'd better hang it over the piano; so we put in some nails and hung it; and it looked very beautiful. Then I hinted that I was thirsty a little bit, and she said she would make us something special. She brought out those tall heavy glasses—like shakers, you know? About a foot high. And filled each one with cracked ice. Then she took brandy and curaçao and red cherries and placed these in the glasses. Then she took a magnum of champagne and poured it over the cracked ice."

"A drink of that potential," I said, "should be named 'The Seven Deadly Virtues'!"

"I don't know what it is called," Paval said, "but the first one went down beautifully. Then we have two; we have three; we have four; and John, he got loaded. By seven o'clock we are ready to go home. And Mark Hellinger has the iron gate, you know; and to open it you have to drive across a cable on the driveway, to work the electric eye. And the funny part of it is that I miss the cable and hit the gate. So here I am afraid to get out of the car, and John said, 'Get me out of this goddam joint!' and I said, 'I'll get you home.'

So I back up, and run all over the thing on the driveway; and the gate opens like the covers of a big monastery book; and I sneak out, and when we get to Alta Loma Drive I have to carry John up the driveway. And that night he had a hemorrhage."

At three o'clock in the morning Phyllis Decker telephoned Paval. "I have to take John to the hospital."

Paval returned to the studio to find a doctor and an ambulance there. "We got him on a stretcher," Paval said. "We got him on the stretcher and carried him down to the ambulance. I followed with Phyllis in my car to the Cedars of Lebanon Hospital. We came up—I think it was the second floor—and they had no room. So John was waiting stretched out in the hallway because—I don't know; they were talking about finances or something that hadn't been arranged. Fanny Brice telephoned the hospital to give John the best room they could manage, and wanted to send John some hot soup. But he couldn't take soup or anything else. So they put him in a room with another guy. Very macabre. The guy was lying there. He was dying. And he had some kind of—he must have had cancer—because it's so vivid in my mind, and he had a drain in his back, and it went pop, pop! You could hear the damn thing. And he said, 'Jesus! I won't be here another minute!' And John said, 'Get me out of here! I can't depend on this man's promise. He might live a whole hour.'"

"All right, John," Paval said, "just take it easy for the rest of the night. Tomorrow you'll be all right."

"The hell I will!" Decker replied. "I wish I could see my creditors' faces when they hear of this."

The doctor administered morphine. At about six o'clock in the morning Decker received the first of the many blood transfusions that were to be given him. Paval stayed on at the hospital until ten o'clock the next morning.

Decker roused once to quote *Cyrano:* " 'It is much finer to fight when it is no use.' "

During the next four weeks Decker spoke again and again of "the Madonna of the Seine." Some months before he had been preoccupied with the retouching of several death masks he had painted at the old studio on Bundy Drive. Paval had made miniature replicas of these in ivory and had set them in rings for Decker. One of the paintings was a copy of Beethoven's death mask; another, that of Sir Walter Scott; still another, the last he had done, was the Madonna of the Seine.

"Just who was this Madonna?" I asked Paval. "Was she a real person? Decker never said."

"Oh yes," Paval replied. "She was very real. She was a young and beautiful girl, and she drowned herself, oh, maybe a century ago; and when she was taken from the water she had a beautiful soft smile on her face, just like the Mona Lisa, and that's why they called her the Madonna of the Seine. She was a Paris girl. Nobody ever knew just who she was; but she was beautiful, and sad, and virginal. And they made a death mask, and it became a must when you went to school in Paris; to learn how to draw you had to make a sketch of the Madonna of the Seine. . . . I sincerely think that John Decker was one of the greatest artists we have ever had. The man was capable of doing anything. . . ."

The one person other than Phyllis and Philip Paval to be allowed to visit Decker was his former neighbor on Bundy Drive, Mrs. Harriet deLaix. She had been a friend of Sadakichi, of Barrymore, of Decker, of Dr. Nolan, and she was my friend. Mrs. deLaix was a graduate nurse, and when Phyllis went one time on a visit to her family in Ohio, Harriet had volunteered to give Decker his insulin shots.

The pirate's chest had been empty for a long time now. Aside from the hospital expense, other debts had accumulated, and Phyllis began to fear that her husband's pictures might be attached by creditors, and taken down from the walls of a Pasadena exhibition that had opened the day after Decker had gone to the hospital.

Ill though he was, Decker managed to smile when he overheard Phyllis mention the possibility of losing the paintings. "Tell my pals to raid the exhibition and hide the pictures."

The artist looked at Mrs. deLaix. "Harriet," he said, "I want you to have one of my pictures. You figure it out; but don't tell my creditors. You may have any one you want."

"Never mind giving me a picture," Harriet said. "Get Phyllis a new hat when you're well."

In other days Decker had selected or designed his wife's hats, and many of her dresses as well. His taste in this respect was excellent. Upon one occasion he visited a milliner's, saw no hats that pleased him, then sketched a hat to be made for Phyllis. He looked on as the hat was being fashioned, took it to his studio, and there painted flowers upon the hatbox.

Harriet visited Decker the day he died. "When I went in, John was sitting up in bed. He had had so many transfusions that there didn't seem to be another vein in his body that would accept the needle. He was very pale and white, and his dark red hair made him seem whiter. And his little mustache had grown out and was very red. He used to touch up his mustache with Phyllis's mascara. And I noticed his profile, and the often-broken nose; but he still was quite handsome, and had the most beautiful strong hands, and a ring on the finger, that Philip Paval had made. A death mask it was—of Beethoven, I think. And John himself looked like a death mask."

" 'Come over close to the bed,' he said to me. 'I want to talk to you, Harriet.'

"I went to him, and he held my hand with the one that was not receiving the transfusion. And his eyes were closed, but he wasn't asleep, and his voice was moderately strong. He was very thin, and I shifted his hand around and secretly took his pulse. It was thready and fast, very fast. That would indicate some internal hemorrhagic condition, as it does in certain surgical cases. I could tell by looking at him that death was close."

She had brought him a little plant, from the ground-cover of her garden, in a small silver dish. It was a mock-strawberry plant, and, unlike the real strawberry vine, bore yellow flowers.

Decker opened his eyes and looked for a moment at this plant, then said, "The blossoms are the same color that Raphael used for the hair of his angels."

Thank you very much. Hah!
    —Sadakichi

We had a few jars of the "craytur," Thomas Mitchell and I, in the hillside shed where I was writing this
book about his old friends and mine. That was in August,
more than a year ago, at the time I saw the blue jay thrust-
ing like a fencing master at the last peach of the season on
a tree in the gully below my window.

August has come again, and is gone. It is September.
Mitchell is back in town from New York, where the versatile
player once again demonstrated his powers on Broadway.
He has been forty years in the theater, has received every high
award, but is a man of such friendly ways that we are apt
to take both the person and the artist for granted, and make
a hero of someone who has but half his talent and twice his
ego.

Mitchell saw new trails down the hill from my arklike
workshed. Now the blue jay had company. Many, many

birds had come here since last summer, among them twenty-eight wild doves. The doves had gone South. They would be resting for a week or so in the Imperial Valley, before flying on to their winter home in Mexico. There was no underbrush now on the glen floor. The trees had been pruned, and the fallen leaves lay in a neat pile for the burning.

"I became so interested in the blue jay," I told Mitchell, "that I had my friend Paul J. Howard, the landscape architect and tree expert, make those trails and clean away the brush. I call the blue jay Sadakichi. He and his wife had a family of three. I used to watch Sadakichi give his children flying lessons. One of the young birds drank all day long at a big stoneware saucer I placed in the glen. The fledgling drank so much that of course you know its name without my telling you."

"W. C. Fields," said Tommy. "Is that a tape recorder I hear running?"

"It is. I get so tired, secretly of course, of having captious persons ask where I get the direct quotes to use in my books that I use the tape recorder whenever possible. Novelist Tom Duncan introduced me to this device. During our days on Bundy Drive, the secretaries took down Barrymore's and Decker's remarks, as well as Sadakichi's."

"We must round up the survivors of that time," Mitchell said, "and have a cocktail party. I don't think that either of us lives in the past, as the term is generally used, but we can't forget the Bundy Drive group."

"In a very special sense," I said, "those men were seeking the Truth."

"You knew Heywood Broun?"

"Very well in my newspaper days."

"Well," Mitchell said, "he would feel sunk, way down sunk at times. Broun would be a socialist tonight, and tomorrow a great one for progress and all that; and he died a Roman Catholic. Nobody seemed to know that the poor guy was trying to say: 'What is the Truth, so far as *I* am concerned?' "

The blue jay I had named Sadakichi heard my voice and now was scolding me from a fence just outside the door. "Don't be so impatient!" I called out to the bird. "I'll feed you as soon as Mitchell tells me what Truth is."

"Now the Truth, so far as you are concerned," Mitchell said, "is not worth a damn as a reality. The Truth is an abstraction. You can say I'm a fellow living in this room—"

"And that may be false tomorrow."

"And false so far as part of you is concerned, the big part of you. The trouble is that you're always trying to let that other big part of you have expression."

"I think," said I, "that each one of us has a built-in Sherlock Holmes who is hunting down the real Mitchell or the real Fowler."

Mitchell was examining some of the many keepsakes I had in my room: Decker's mailbox, Barrymore's brown belt, Jack Dempsey's battered valise, the one he had carried long ago as a young prizefighter.

Tommy picked up a cocktail glass that had a twisted stem and a canted bowl. "What's this? Part of the Laocoön group copied in glass?"

"Sadakichi gave it to me," I said. "Melted the thing over a gas jet one night at Decker's. He held it in his bare hands while heating it, mind you, and never got so much as a blister."

"He was a cynic," Mitchell said. "So definitely a cynic."

"Perhaps," I said. "His words had teeth, even though he hadn't any. But I sometimes suspected him of a soft spot or two."

"No. He was a cynic, a fellow who got burned too soon. That's why Sadakichi didn't blister when he reshaped this glass. He'd already been burned beyond all effect of mere fire. And he was reshaping the world, in his own eerie imagination, when he twisted this glass." He put down the glass, then looked at a reliquary in which some cinders lay. "What's this? Not Decker's ashes?"

"Ashes of the Abbey Theatre," I said. "From the stage apron. The Abbey people gave these ashes to me when I was in Dublin, the day after fire destroyed the old theater."

"The Abbey people have been the most dedicated playwrights and actors of our time."

"They also gave me the prompt book of *Juno and the Paycock,* all water-logged and singed, as you see. It was salvaged, together with some other things, from the green room."

"They are nice people."

"Well, I never did anything for the Abbey Theatre except admire it. One of the pretty actresses asked me to pardon her for not shaking hands. She had burned them while trying to save costumes in the wardrobe room. Yet she appeared that same night in *The Plough and the Stars* at the little Peacock Theatre next door to the Abbey."

Mitchell now examined a pair of small opera glasses,

mounted on temples, to be worn at the theater as one does eyeglasses. "These are Jack's?"

"Yes, Barrymore liked to sit far back in the audience—"

"Most actors do," Mitchell interrupted. "But Jack also could slip out for a quick one unobserved. Nor would he cause any disturbance that might distract attention from the play. He had a most meticulous regard for the art of acting and for the staging of a play."

Mitchell recalled the time in 1918 when he appeared with Barrymore in *Redemption*. "I didn't come on-stage until ten o'clock each evening. I had a long scene with Jack, a very important one for the understanding of the part he was playing. One night I was amazed when he began to cut his own lines and to speed up the scene with me. No matter how careless he may have been with his life, he was a martinet on-stage, and if anyone was in the least deficient in a scene with him, slow with the cue lines, or slovenly in delivery, he would blast that person as only he knew how to do. But tonight he left out great chunks of the dialogue and kept whispering to me, 'Are you all right, old man?' After the final curtain he came to my dressing room to ask again if I was feeling all right. I said of course I was, and what the hell? And he seemed greatly relieved as he said, 'I thought I smelled booze on your breath as we began our scene.' I told him I had had exactly one martini before going on, no more, no less. He smiled. 'Oh, I was afraid you were drunk; and that's the only fault I can forgive in an actor. I merely wanted to take the strain off you.'"

"Jack should have been there to protect Decker the night he opened and closed in Greenwich Village and fell into the orchestra pit. You were at the Decker funeral, as I remember?"

"Yes. And it was indeed a Decker production. He had asked to be laid out on the bar of the new studio, but Phyllis would have none of that. There were folding chairs placed for the convenience of his friends as they looked on and listened to the phonograph recording Decker had made of the 'No, I thank you!' speech from *Cyrano*."

"Do you have any idea why he was so fond of that speech?" It's the one in which Cyrano gives a "no thanks" to his self-posed idea of cringing before some grandee patron or groveling at the feet of fame.

"Well, what seemed to fascinate our friend," Mitchell replied, "was that part of Cyrano which defied convention, just as Decker himself always did. In reality, Decker was saying, 'If you expect me to be a pedestrian fellow who will live to be eighty merely to collect my insurance—no thank you, sir. If you think I'm going to come home every night to a sweet little woman who expects me to act out her small vision of the dutiful fellow she thought I was when we were married—no thank you, madam. If you expect me to quit spending the thousand dollars I do not have, and exchange my wild dreams and desires for a tame but safe existence in the assembly line—no thank you!' "

"I was too ill to be there," I said. "But I was told that the wreath I sent fell during the recitation. Some persons, my son Will for one, said that Barrymore's picture also fell from the wall."

"Barrymore's picture fell. Maybe the wreath too. It was a macabre occurrence. That picture—I think Jimmy Mc-

Hugh has it now—came loose from the wall as the last 'no thank you' sounded. A wreath, whether or not it was yours, was on an easel that also held John's last still-life, a wonderful thing called 'The Yellow Book.' A picture of a barn hung just back of the easel. By the way, what happened to Decker's ashes?"

"Phyllis tried to interest the cemetery people in placing them in the Hall of Honor, or whatever it's called, at Forest Lawn. The head man out there declined to do this, and wrote a letter to Dr. Valentiner, and sent a copy of it to me, saying that Gutzon Borglum and Carrie Jacobs Bond were buried there—"

"Those two worthies," Mitchell interrupted, "wouldn't understand Decker; but they might learn to endure him, in eternal time."

"The gentleman in charge," I said, "claimed in this letter that the Hall-of-Whatever-It-Is is known as the Westminster Abbey of America."

"I'm glad to hear that," Mitchell said. "But what about the ashes?"

"There was some talk of the rent not having been paid on them at the mortuary."

"How like Decker! Always behind in the rent."

"And now it seems the ashes are, in a sense, lost. But efforts are being made to locate them."

Mitchell thought for a moment, then said, "But his fame will not be lost. One day his work, too little of it perhaps, but some six or seven of his pictures, is bound to be recognized as among the finest of modern times."

Mitchell said that on the day of the funeral, in June of

1947, he had been doing a motion-picture with Errol Flynn at the Warner Brothers Studio. Both actors obtained leave of absence to be present at the services and then went back to Burbank.

"When the camera work was over for the day," Mitchell said, "I returned to the almost empty place on Alta Loma Drive. Phyllis was there, waiting while a young man from the chair-rental company folded and carried away the chairs. The picture of the barn, which I now own, seemed to catch the young man's eye. He paused in his work to look at the picture for several long moments.

"Now I don't think this young fellow knew a painting from a colored print. Something he had said indicated that he had been born on a farm in the Middle West. He turned from the picture and said matter-of-factly to Phyllis, 'The door of the barn is on the wrong side.'

"Phyllis looked at the picture, as though for the first time, then said slowly, 'Yes, I think it is.' It was as if Phyllis suddenly had left a world in which she had lived for some years with the artist and among his friends; and now, as a former child of the farmlands, suddenly had been called back to the things of the soil by someone of her own way of thinking and of living in her girlhood days. Until now it seemed as though she had seen this barn, as well as all other things, as Decker had seen them. Now, with the emptiness that Decker's death had brought, his eyes no longer were hers as well; and she saw the world as the world saw itself."

Mitchell again expressed the desire to have a cocktail party for the "survivors."

"*What* survivors?" I asked.

The actor seemed almost stunned by my question. "You know, it's incredible! So many have gone. How stupid of me even to think of a party. We'd have to call the undertaker to find out which people, if any, he hasn't put away. There must be a law against us having any living friends."

"Tommy," I said, "I think we'll have to wait till Judgment Day to give our party."

"Tell me," he said, "did our friends die young, or is it merely that we are getting old and don't know it?"

"You and I are convalescents."

"Meaning what?"

"We are recovering from a disease called Youth."

Tommy went home, and I took some scratch grain down to the birds, and wondered if the doves were happy in the Imperial Valley and when they would be flying South.

A bonfire of tree leaves smells sweet in the autumn air; and an old man, watching the gray smoke rise, leans on his rake and thinks of winter.

W. C. Fields as "Victoria Regina," painted by
John Decker

Hartmann dancing the Tarantella (with variations), as sk[...]
by Decker

John Decker's po[...]
of his wife, Phyll[...]

Hartmann dancing "The Cossack's Gavotsky," as
sketched by Decker